transcendent s

gamba

baby was an issue

Imperial Valley Nisei Women: Transcending Poston

Second Printing, February, 2007

Design and Illustrations: Elizabeth Percival
Printed by Eastwood Litho Inc., Syracuse, NY

$23.95

 Published in the United States of America in Syracuse, New York by New Persephone Press.

For information concerning this book write to:
New Persephone Press, 4465 E. Genesee Street, PMB 183, Dewitt, NY 13214, U.S.A.
Email: newpersephonepress@twcny.rr.com

Imperial Valley Nisei Women: Transcending Poston

To Linda — a kindred ARCOA'N
May some of these life stories inspire you.
Warmest wishes —

Joan Loveridge-Sanbonmatsu

Joan Loveridge-Sanbonmatsu
5/20/2012

new persephone press

in conjunction with

Japanese American Citizens League
Imperial Valley Chapter
and
Imperial County Historical Society
Pioneers' Museum

DEDICATION

To the Japanese Americans

from Imperial Valley who were

interned at Poston I Camp and to all

Japanese Americans who were interned in camps during World War II

and to those who also served

in the Armed Forces, who live,

and who died with *gambaru.*

CONTENTS

PREFACE

Wellsprings for this book pulsated from several grants in the 1980's and 1990's. The University of Illinois at Chicago awarded me a summer fellowship to participate in the Multicultural Women's Summer Institute directed by Dr. Margaret Strobel and State University of New York at Oswego supported me with a travel grant. That summer I learned the value of oral histories and conducted my first oral history with Ruri Tsuchiya Ishimaru in Chicago. Further, I made my first trip to the National Archives in Washington, DC. Encouraged by historian Dr. Judith Wellman, I did many oral histories (more than thirty-five) and integrated the concept and practice into my Intercultural Communication course at SUNY Oswego for fifteen years.

In 1994, I was the recipient of a SUNY Oswego Research Enhancement Grant to conduct oral histories of Japanese American women in Imperial Valley, California who had been interned at Poston I Camp during World War II. Included in this group was the original tape recorded oral history interview of Tsuchiya Ishimaru and four interviewees, ages fifteen to twenty-eight in camp: Mabel Kawashima Ota; Mary Shigematsu Hoshizaki; Mary Mitamura Sanbonmatsu; and Yoshiko Mitamura Kodama. All lived in Imperial Valley. I took this opportunity to conduct more interviews with Tsuchiya Ishimaru. Importantly, I made many trips to the Cornell University Poston Collection of thirty-nine boxes of research materials on the Poston I Camp. This research informed my development of interview questions.

Basic questions were given in writing to the interviewees ahead so that they could review dates and names, if they wanted. Examples of the questions follow:

1. What stories did your mother and father pass on to you?
2. Your growing up years—tell us about them?
3. What were the turning points in your life?
4. Was camp a yardstick for the rest of your life?
5. What were some of the issues in camp?
   Milk, dust storms, strikes? (Before my research at Cornell, for instance, I didn't know that dust storms were horrendous and everyone had much to say about them.)
6. What were some of your family's values?
7. What were the roles of women and men at camp?
8. What were the communication patterns at camp?
9. What were the issues of discrimination?
10. At what point did you move beyond camp?
11. Tell us about life after camp.
12. What message do you have for future generations?

Questions were adapted to the situation of the particular interviewee. For example, Mary Mitamura was the only high school student in the group, so some questions were tailored to her experiences in high school and the high school curriculum and education in camp.

The questions and their responses were then clustered into the following groups:

1. Growing up years and stories passed on.
2. Issues of discrimination and gender equity.
3. Turning points in lives.
4. Issues in camp of birthing, childcare and health.
5. Roles, values, education and communication patterns in camp.
6. Using camp as a yardstick.
7. Moving beyond camp and issues of resettlement.
8. Life today.

All of the interviews were tape recorded with the exception of Mary Shigematsu Hoshizaki. With her interview, I took detailed notes. All of the tape recorded interviews were carefully transcribed by Betty Restuccia, an experienced transcriber.

In 1996-1997, the first drafts of the book began. During my sabbatical I visited Poston Camp I in Parker, Arizona, the Imperial County Historical Society Pioneers' Museum, having been to several Poston Japanese American Reunions, the California State University at Fullerton Oral History Program, the Japanese American National Museum in Los Angeles and many conferences. Over the years some of the conferences in which I participated follow: New York Asian Studies, the American Historical Association, National Communication Association (NCA), Ethnography Conference in Chicago sponsored by the NCA, Speech Communication Association of Puerto Rico, National Women's Studies Association, all of which had programs on the Japanese American experience.

During the writing of the manuscript, I had follow-up interviews and conversations with all the interviewees to check facts and gather more detailed information. Conferences were held with all of the interviewees except for Tsuchiya Ishimaru who passed away, to go over their chapters. Her son and daughter-in-law, Mikio and Vickie Ishimaru read the chapter of Tsuchiya Ishimaru.

Gathering photos for the book was an ongoing process. Most of the photos were loaned or given to me by the families. Cameras were banned in the camps; hence the camp photos are rare.

The purposes of this book are to facilitate the telling of inspiring stories of these five remarkable women from Imperial Valley, California; to document their stories of courage and determination in confronting physical and emotional hardships, racial and gender discrimination, language barriers and wartime *concentration camps* in the United States.* Resettlement after the camps meant extreme losses of property, housing and finances. Lastly, the voices of these five women give us messages today for future generations.

**Concentration camps* are not to be confused with the death camps in Europe in World War II.

Acknowledgements

Above all, my deepest gratitude goes to the interviewees: Mabel Kawashima Ota; Mary Shigematsu Hoshizaki; Ruri Tsuchiya Ishimaru; Yoshiko Mitamura Kodama; Mary Mitamura Sanbonmatsu and to their families who provided photos and additional information. Without their involvement, this project would not have been possible.

Akira Loveridge-Sanbonmatsu for his special gifts of unfailing support, listening ear, profound memory of his Poston Internment, editing and much more.

James Michael Sanbonmatsu whose work with low income housing and whose imaginative stories, photography, and songwriting for his band, Sweet Polly Purebred, spur me on.

Kevin Yosh Sanbonmatsu who continues to inspire me with the excitement of his scientific research and to lend his infinite patience and command of computers.

Rosabel A. Wang, whose expertise in the field of publishing, editing and problem-solving is incomparable.

Elizabeth Percival, designer and artist extraordinaire.

Nancy Seale Osborne, kindred writer, for her perceptive editing, careful proofing and continuing support over the years.

Laurie A. Smith, photographer, who generously contributed her time and talent in taking over one hundred excellent copy photos for the project and for teaching me an accessioning and cataloging system for all the photos.

Mitsuye Yamada, poet, activist and friend whose ideas and poetry have enriched my life.

Tim Asamen of Imperial Valley for his thoughtful questions, information, and recommendations.

Barbara J. Bruegger, Sharon Lee Foote Cann, Lucie Davidson, Bobbie A. Casey McHale, Cindy Oliphant Meadows, Jan Olin Miller, Evelyn Matheson Styan, Mary P. Sullivan O'Driscoll, Barbara A. Mace Otaki, Kathryn Undercoffer, Martha Undercoffer, Anita Wright and all my American Red Cross Overseas Association friends for their early confidence in this book.

Joan Carroll for her valued advice.

Pat Cullinan for her time consciousness and skilled computer work.

Joan M. Fayer, University of Puerto Rico at Rio Piedras, for her illuminating dialogue about ethnography.

Yoshiko Fujita-Butler for her gracious willingness and creativity in penning the calligraphy and translation of the haiku into *Romanji* along with Hiromi Kubo and Keita Matsubara.

Candice Funakoshi for her kindness in helping me with checking facts.

Barbara Gerber for her wise counsel.

Nola Heidlebaugh, Judith Martin, Marcia Moore, Fritz Messere and John Kares Smith for their empathetic ear and esteemed friendship.

Jason Jackson from Imperial Valley for his enthusiasm and commitment to the project.

Mark Knopp, creative photographer, whose experience and goodwill have added to the project.

Marsha Kroll, David Mook and Burnham Holmes, Vermont poets and writers, for their encouragement and important conversations about this book and all my Vermont friends including Sue Claire Bachelder, Linda Nye Barbaro, Ann Rich Duncan, Brian and Karen Festa, Pam and Richard Green, Bob and Marlene Isherwood and Joyce McGreevy.

Barbara Kwasnik for her professional knowledge and help.

Librarians and their staffs for their invaluable assistance in locating significant documents at Cornell University Archives, California State University at Fullerton Oral History Library, National Archives, Penfield Library at SUNY Oswego, Griswold Library at Green Mountain College. Of special note are Mignon Adams, Sharon Lee Foote Cann, Blanche Judd, Paul Millette and his excellent and hospitable staff, Gail Schaumloffel, Cadence Atchinson, Raina Robins, Ken Coe and Lisa Nelson, and Nancy Seale Osborne.

Masumi Nyui for instructive clarifications.

Bill Reilly and Mindy Ostrow, owners of the river's end bookstore in Oswego, New York for their energy, know-how, nurturance of writers and community, giving opportunities for readings and active exchanges of ideas.

Betty Restuccia for her steadfast typing and technical editing of the early drafts of this book, her many careful transcriptions of oral histories over twenty-five years and her friendship.

Yoshiya, Bruce Sanbonmatsu and Mary Mitamura Sanbonmatsu for warm hospitality in Imperial Valley.

Barbara St. Michel for her insightful suggestions.

Heartfelt appreciation for consultation goes to Eves, my cherished women's group; Imperial County Historical Society Pioneers' Museum; Imperial Valley Japanese American Gallery; Japanese American Citizens League—Imperial Valley Chapter; Multicultural Women's Summer Institute at the University of Illinois at Chicago; National Japanese American Citizens League; State University of New York at Oswego Communication Studies Department, the Women's Studies Program and the Intensive English Program; State University of New York at Oswego for Faculty Research Enhancement Grants and a sabbatical leave which provided time and support to conduct the interviews and to write early drafts of this book.

Stone Ishimaru, acclaimed Poston photographer, for his excellent photos.

Photo Credits

Copy Photos.. Laurie A. Smith—photos throughout the book.

Photos of Mary Shigematsu Hoshizaki .... Jason Jackson, pages 27, 29.

Photo of Jason Jackson ....Joan Loveridge-Sanbonmatsu, 28.

Photo of Mary Mitamura Sanbonmatsu and dog .... James Michael Sanbonmatsu, 39.

Photo of Mary Mitamura Sanbonmatsu,
and Yoshiya Sanbonmatsu and dogs .... Bruce Sanbonmatsu, 40.

Photo of Sanbon, Inc...Joan Loveridge-Sanbonmatsu, 41.

Photo of Yoshiko Kodama .... George Kodama, 53.

Photo of Ruri Tsuchiya Ishimaru and Tsukumo Ishimaru.........................Joan Loveridge-Sanbonmatsu, 67.

Photo of Joan Loveridge-Sanbonmatsu...Mark Knopp, 89.

Camp photos of Poston.. Stone Ishimaru.

Haiku, Calligraphy and Translation Credits

Strong Japanese tree For Mabel Kawashima Ota .... 6.
By Joan Loveridge-Sanbonmatsu
Calligraphy: Yoshiko Fujita-Butler
Translation: Yoshiko Fujita-Butler and Hiromi Kubo

Only at desert camp For Mabel Kawashima Ota .... 19.
By Joan Loveridge-Sanbonmatsu
Calligraphy: Yoshiko Fujita-Butler
Translation: Yoshiko Fujita-Butler and Hiromi Kubo

When cottonwood trees For Ruri Tsuchiya Ishimaru .... 54.
By Joan Loveridge-Sanbonmatsu
Calligraphy: Keita Matsubara, Tsukuba University
Translation: Yoshiko Fujita-Butler and Hiromi Kubo

PROFILES

Mabel Kawashima Ota, Los Angeles
Eighty-nine years of age
Born September 18, 1916 in San Diego
Nisei, Raised in Calexico, California
Camp: Poston I, Arizona—April 1942-November 1943
Block 6
    New York City—November 1943-April 1944
Poston I, Block 5
    April 1944-June 1944

Mabel Kawashima Ota, raised in Calexico in Imperial Valley, graduated Valedictorian from Calexico Union High School where she won debate tournaments, starred in the junior-senior play, *Dutch Detective,* and played on the tennis team. At UCLA, Mabel Kawashima Ota majored in sociology. In 1940, she married Fred Ota. As early volunteers, Fred and Mabel went to camp in April 1942: she to set up a library and Fred to run the canteen. Madeline, their first baby, was born in camp. Candice, their second child, was born after camp in 1947 in Los Angeles.

Mabel Kawashima Ota completed her Master's Degree in Education and became one of the first Japanese American teachers in the Los Angeles City School District and the first Asian woman principal in California. When she retired from the principalship, she was elected Senior Assemblywoman. She became a member of the Council on Aging, and chaired the Advocacy Committee, serving twenty years. "If you want something changed in society, it has to be done through the legal process," she advised. Now, she is involved in the Seinan Japanese American Senior Center.

Mabel Kawashima Ota described herself as "goal oriented since her freshman year in high school and very religious." She is "guided by God," and has taught Sunday school since her junior year in high school.

Mary Shigematsu Hoshizaki, El Centro
Eighty-three years of age on February 27, 2001
Born May 1, 1917 in Dayton, New Mexico; deceased February 27, 2001, El Centro, California
Nisei, Raised in Imperial and El Centro, California
Camp: Poston I, Arizona—1942-1945
Block 60

Mary Shigematsu Hoshizaki grew up in Imperial Valley, and graduated from Central High in El Centro, from Woodbury College where she majored in Costume Arts and Illustration. She married George Hoshizaki on October 23, 1937. When she entered camp, her oldest daughter, Marilyn, was one and a half years old, and baby Carolyn was eight months old. Her son, Wayne, was born in camp.

After Poston, Mary, an outgoing woman, worked for the Pan American Underwriters Insurance Agency in El Centro where "she was one of the first women to wear slacks in the office." She worked in the areas of Workers Compensation and Claims Adjustment. A strong and can-do trailblazer, Mary Shigematsu Hoshizaki was the first woman in the San Diego area to break the male barrier in deep-sea fishing. She was well known at all the landings and especially Fisherman's Landing. She and her husband, George Hoshizaki, who passed away February 9, 1993, her son, Wayne, and grandson, Jason, used to fish big time. She filleted the fish and canned the tuna. A number of years ago, Mary Shigematsu Hoshizaki competed to get into the Yellow Tail Derby in San Diego; she qualified. And in that Yellow Tail Derby she won first place: a new car. A good negotiator, she traded the car, since she already had one, for an air conditioning system for her home.

At age eighty, Mary Shigematsu Hoshizaki caught a ninety pound Blue Fin Tuna on the boat, Pacific Queen. To her, "fishing was a great stress reliever." Then, Mary Shigematsu Hoshizaki, at age eighty, launched a new career preparing sushi in a sushi bar called the Arigato Sushi Bar in an El Centro café where she worked part-time. In addition, she was a crafter, whose creativity was seen in quilting and other arts. Most importantly though, Mary Shigematsu Hoshizaki served as Treasurer of the Japanese American Citizens League, Imperial Valley Chapter.

Mary Mitamura Sanbonmatsu, Holtville, California
Seventy-nine years of age
Nisei, Born November 20, 1926 in Imperial, California
Camp: Poston I, Arizona—1942-1945
Block 39

Mary Mitamura Sanbonmatsu graduated from Poston High School in camp where she was on the basketball team and served as business manager for the Poston High Yearbook called *Post-Año.* Mary Mitamura was described as "personality plus, plus," "personality, beauty, brains plus," "the most agreeable companion—one who would not have you any different than you are—that's Mary."

After camp, when Mary Mitamura worked for an insurance company in Los Angeles, her boss asked if she had any Japanese American women friends who worked as hard as she did. Mary Mitamura reconnected with Yoshiya Sanbonmatsu whom she had met in camp, and soon they married. She moved back to the valley [Imperial Valley] along with Yoshiya where her son, Bruce, was born. Mary Mitamura Sanbonmatsu, Yoshiya Sanbonmatsu, and son, Bruce, run the family business, Sanbon, Incorporated.

"Dynamic, vivacious and energetic," Mary describes herself. Reflecting on her life, she asserts, "Life pushes you to do your best and to do the best you can every day, whether in Sanbon, Inc., or otherwise."

Yoshiko Mitamura Kodama, El Centro, California
Eighty-three years of age
Nisei, Born March 11, 1923 in Imperial Valley, California
Camp: Poston I, Arizona—1942-1944
Block 39

Yoshiko (Yosh) Mitamura attended Imperial High School and Imperial Valley Junior College. Yosh Mitamura and George Kodama married in camp in 1943. After Poston, she moved back to the valley with George, where she worked for the State Department of Human Resources and was responsible for unemployment and job searches. After working many years for the state, Yosh Mitamura Kodama retired, and now works for Sanbon, Inc., along with two of her three children Diane and Craig. Currently, her son Glenn has moved into Custom Services in Vancouver.

Active in the Japanese American Citizens League, Imperial Valley Chapter, Mitamura Kodama now serves as its treasurer. She "feels very blessed in her life in all aspects—health and family wise."

Ruri Tsuchiya Ishimaru
Born June 24, 1913 in San Fransisco, California—died July 16, 1997, Chicago, Illinois
Kibei, Educated in Japan
Camp: Poston I, Arizona—1942-1945
Block 39

Ruri Tsuchiya Ishimaru, from the age of three, was educated in Japan, graduating from the Girls High School in Chiba-Ken near Tokyo, and Tokyo Women's College. She returned to the United States at age 19 to help care for her five brothers after their father died. At age 20, Ruri Tsuchiya taught Japanese classes and at age 22, she began writing articles for the Los Angeles based national Japanese newspaper, the *Rafu Shimpo.*

An independent and nurturing woman, Ruri drove a car and stood up for the rights of Japanese American women. In her columns, she asserted that women should be able to dance and to wear makeup and pants, if they chose. Shortly after she married Tsukumo Ishimaru, at age 28, they were evacuated to Poston I where she had baby Mikio in January 1943. Upon leaving camp, they moved to New York City and then to Chicago. On July 16, 1997, Ruri Tsuchiya Ishimaru was struck down, at age 84, by a Chicago Transit bus at Lawrence and Foster streets outside Heiwa Terrace, her apartment building in Chicago. She was returning home from visiting her husband, Tsukumo Ishimaru, who had had a stroke and was at the Harmony Nursing and Rehabilitation Home.

KEY

o ASSEMBLY CENTERS

Puyallup, Wash.
Portland, Ore.
Marysville, Calif.
Sacramento, Calif.
Tanforan, Calif.
Stockton, Calif.
Turlock, Calif.
Merced, Calif.
Pinedale, Calif.
Salinas, Calif.
Fresno, Calif.
Tulare, Calif.
Santa Anita, Calif.
Pomona, Calif.
Mayer, Ariz.

■ RELOCATION CENTERS

Manzanar, Calif.
Tule Lake, Calif.
Poston, Ariz.
Gila, Ariz.
Minidoka, Ida.
Heart Mountain, Wyo.
Granada, Colo.
Topaz, Utah
Rohwer, Ark.
Jerome, Ark.

• JUSTICE DEPARTMENT INTERNMENT CAMPS

Santa Fe, N. Mex.
Bismarck, N. Dak.
Crystal City, Tex.
Missoula, Mont.

Δ CITIZEN ISOLATION CAMPS

Moab, Utah
Leupp, Ariz.

Military Area 2 or
"Free Zone" until March 29, 1942

Map from Nishiura Weglyn, *Years of Infamy*

Introduction

SELDOM HAS THE United States history been marred with such blind racism as was evident by the imprisonment of all Japanese Americans on the West Coast during World War II. More than 110,000 Japanese and Japanese Americans in the United States were rounded up and put into internment camps. Several thousand young, sick, and elderly along with the able-bodied Japanese Americans were given less than 48 hours to sell their houses, farms, pack the few belongings they could carry, and give away their dogs and cats. For three and a half or four years, teenagers spent their high school years in camp; others became of age, married, bore their first babies; got their first jobs in camp; saw their parents become ill and die. The shunning before camp and during the resettlement after camp was painful; the loss of their family homes, their friends, jobs, and community became the uprooting of a generation. Bitterness, depression, and illness grew like cancer while their potential for resiliancy and unlimited growth coursed through them. Many Japanese Americans measured their lives by camp.

Testimony of this was given by Dr. Lucie C. Hirata on behalf of the UCLA Asian American Studies Center before the Commission on Wartime Relocation and Internment of Civilians in 1981. She cited Dr. Don T. Nakanishi who stated that "the psychological effects of the concentration camps are similar to those which have been observed among survivors of other major historical tragedies and disasters such as the Hiroshima atomic bombings and the Holocaust. These enduring psychological effects include the following: loss of self-confidence concerning personal invulnerability; a profound and complex inner struggle between remembering and forgetting the event; guilt and shame; heightened personal anxiety; and a continual use of the event as a 'frame of reference' for assessing life events before and after the tragedy. It was a profoundly traumatic event which Japanese Americans have had to 'survive' at considerable psychological costs."[1]

After Japan bombed Pearl Harbor in December 1941, President Franklin Delano Roosevelt declared war and two months later signed Executive Order 9066 ordering a mass removal of some 110,000 Japanese and Japanese Americans in Washington, Oregon, California, and Arizona from the West Coast. Transports were sent to the interior in such states as Arizona, Idaho, California, Wyoming, Colorado, Utah, and Arkansas.

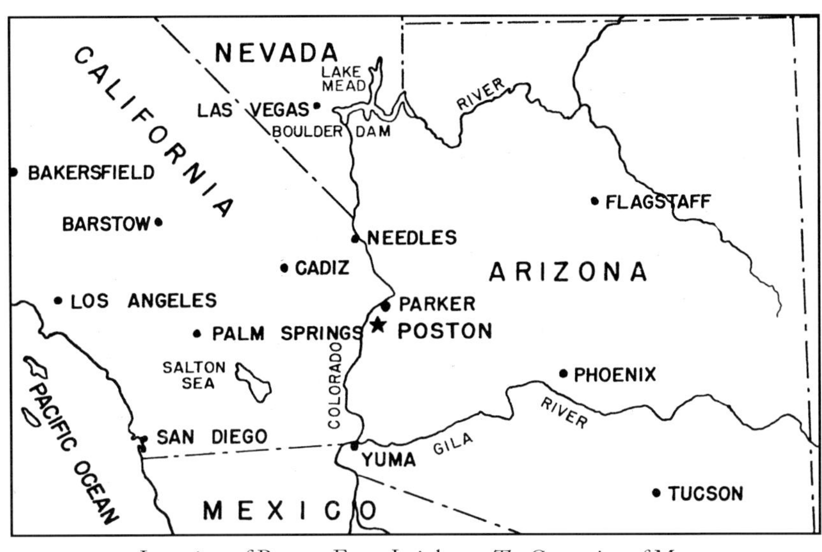

Location of Poston. From Leighton, *The Governing of Men*

Col. Karl Bendetsen of the Western Defense Command asserted, "I am determined that if there is one drop of Japanese blood in them, they must go to camp." As Hirabayashi and Hirabayashi point out in their essay, "Behind Barbed Wire," "The public policy of mass incarceration was directed solely at persons of Japanese descent, despite the fact that America was also at war with Italy and Germany. Moreover, Japanese Hawaiians were never subjected to mass incarceration, although Hawaii was more susceptible to invasion."[2]

Poston Established on Native American Reservation

Ten camps were established with one of the largest being Poston, located on a Native American reservation in Parker, Arizona in the middle of a desert with temperatures ranging from 30°F to 136°F.[3] Poston was one of the first camps to be built and divided into three camps. The poignant stories you will read are of five Japanese American Nisei* women at Poston in their own unforgettable words, juxtapositioned to some observations made by a Native American woman. These five women from Imperial Valley bore witness to this miscarriage of justice. No other books exist which focus solely on Imperial Valley Nisei women interned in Poston using oral histories in their own words. These five women came from one of the most agricultural areas in the country, Imperial Valley. Not only did they live in Imperial Valley, but importantly and courageously, most returned to the Imperial Valley area after camp, only to face racial harassment, threats to their lives, and unwelcoming communities. There had been a ban on returning to the West Coast. Although this ban was lifted on January 2, 1945, the government urged people not to return to specific counties, such as Imperial County, not to congregate in large groups, and to make every attempt not to appear prominent.

Observations by Agnes Savilla, a Mojave, reveal another dimension of Poston and Parker, the reservation, and the Native peoples who lived there. Parker is a small town in the desert of Arizona whose population is a small 7,000 people. Poston was built just outside of Parker. When it was announced that a camp was being built, her reaction was: "The white man is treating them like he treated us." It was a total

*Nisei are second generation Japanese Americans born in the United States as citizens.

surprise. Agnes Savilla in an oral history told this story: "At that time I was working with the Indian Tribal Council. I was coming out of the agency office at about five o'clock when Mr. Gensler, the superintendent said, 'There's a council meeting tomorrow isn't there?' I said, 'Yes.' He said, 'I just had a call from San Francisco, and they're bringing 20,000 Japanese in here.' I looked at him and said, 'Well, why?' He asked, 'What do you think the council will think of it?' I said, 'They won't like it!' You see, we knew nothing about it."[4]

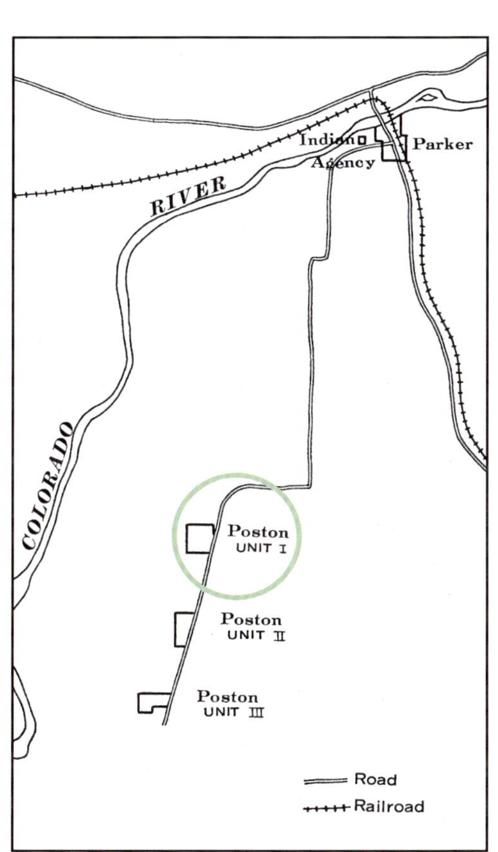

Poston I. From Leighton, *The Governing of Men*

Two tribes, Mojave and the Chemehuevis, lived on the reservation, then the Colorado Indian Tribes, "united in their stand against the government." Agnes Savilla concurred when she said, "Yes, against the government, not the Japanese."[5]

Savilla asserted that the Native peoples "lost the use of that land."[6] "We had some people up here that were very bitter against the Japanese. I remember seeing signs up," Savilla commented.[7] "I remember a remark made, 'Well, I guess now we'll have Japanese relatives in here."[8] The Native peoples were told they had lost the southern end of the reservation.[9] Residents of the community of Parker were angry at the building of camps in their vicinity.[10] People resented that they had to pay for their food, housing, and living expenses.

Nevertheless, bicultural exchanges with the Japanese Americans were established during the National Indian Days. Some Japanese Americans went horseback riding once in a while.[11] Moreover, students engaged in sports competitions.

"When the war ended, the barracks that were built here were sold to many Indians living in the valley," according to David A. Hacker, interviewer of Agnes Savilla.[12]

Indeed, the environment was a very complex situation into which the Japanese Americans were forced. Against the backdrop of hysteria and racism, however, there are stories of bonding, courage, and intense times. "Oral histories," according to Arthur A. Hansen at the Fullerton, California Oral History program, "can be used as a corrective and supplement to existing sources." They can "uncover new problems for consideration" and "convey how people felt."[13]

Imperial Valley

Our stories begin in Imperial Valley which lies in a corner of California near the border of Mexico. One can see in the valley spectacular sunsets framed by tall palm trees blowing in the wind. In the valley, desert lands have been transformed into rich farmlands; pioneering families from Japan settled here but were unexpectedly and suddenly uprooted and evacuated after Pearl Harbor.

Here in the valley, four interviewees as girls grew up in Imperial, Holtville, Calexico and El Centro, small towns down in the valley; all lived there. Holtville's town square is bordered by the library, and the welcome sign sways on the Chamber of Commerce building. In the early 1940s, the teenagers would hang out at the two movie theaters—one indoor, and one outdoor theater, or at the ice cream fountain. Saturday nights would be spent going to a movie or a school dance. On Sundays, the girls might go to El Centro to the Japanese Christian Church, Buddhist Temple, or the First Christian Church in Holtville. Holtville was a farming town of 1,700 people.

"I was home cooking dinner and heard the news on the radio," remembered Ruri Tsuchiya Ishimaru. "Right after Pearl Harbor, I think [in] the Los Angeles area, the coast people started moving. People had to move within 24 hours on the West Coast." [Probably refers to Terminal Island.]

These are the life stories of five young women from Imperial Valley—Mabel Kawashima Ota, Mary Shigematsu Hoshizaki, Mary Mitamura Sanbonmatsu, Yoshiko Mitamura Kodama, and Ruri Tsuchiya Ishimaru, interned at Poston Camp, Arizona during World War II, 1941-1945. Their moving stories help us understand more deeply the experiences and feelings of Japanese American Nisei women before the uprooting and evacuation to Arizona, and in camp, how women thought about Poston in more than one way, the meanings they made out of their experiences, and what the immense costs of the experience were. Poston subjected internees to freezing winters, blistering summers, and ferocious dust storms. We will discover some women's roles in camp, how women saw themselves, questions of value and how relationships diminished life or enriched life. We will see how women's perceptions affected their understanding of themselves and ways in which some women were conflicted in their feelings. Above all, we will see how these valley women overcame living behind barbed wire and how most dared to return to California or the West Coast after camp; how they discovered their voices, identified turning points in their lives, the epiphanies they learned, the strengths they gained to transcend camp, and how they moved ahead to build successful new lives in a country still fraught with discrimination and prejudice.

These stories are opportunities to revalue women's perspectives, to render their oral histories accessible to the public, to reveal experiences in less edited form, and to hear what women implied or started to say but didn't—things left unsaid. Their secrets of resiliency and transcendent spirits are uncovered.

A completed section of Poston. From Leighton, *The Governing of Men*

"There was a Nisei vocabulary based on one deep common experience of World War II: *camp.* Camp was the password, evocative of barbed wire and barracks, desert exile, and war. 'Tule Lake,' 'Poston,' and 'Topaz' indicated not merely location but a state of being," according to Valeri Matsumoto.[14]

These women lived the injustices, alienation, and humiliation of camp, as well as teenagers' bittersweet memories of Friday night dances, the basketball games and high school graduation. We will read about the resettlement difficulties—economic, securing a job, discrimination and family problems. We will hear Mabel Kawashima Ota's story of heartbreaking childbirth, the tragic misdiagnosis of her father's illness, and the courage required to confront these tough times. The events of her life will remain with the reader long after the book has been finished.

Through these experiences, we will discover crises in camp: birthing, medical care and health, and childcare; the quality of life; communication patterns, roles, values and education; issues of discrimination and gender equity; utilization of camp as a yardstick to measure the rest of their lives; moving on beyond camp, including the aftermath of resettlement; turning points in their lives and the family stories passed on.

Strong Japanese tree
bends with wind without breaking
flaming red maple

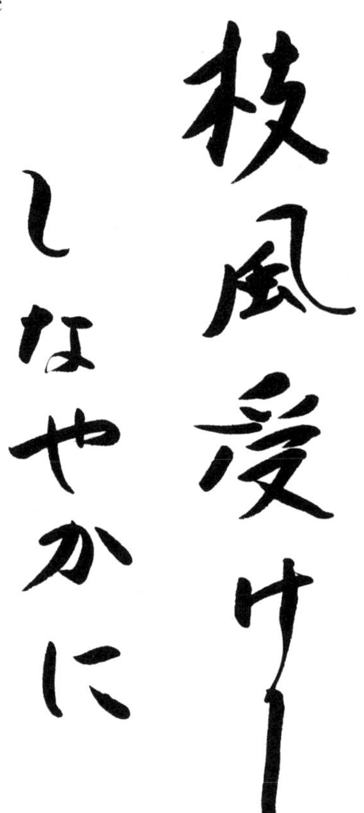

Ku-re-na-i no
e-da ka-ze u-ke-shi
shi-na-ya-ka-ni

MABEL KAWASHIMA OTA'S STORY

"If I can get through camp and what it dealt me, I can get through anything."

Poston, an abandoned mine, sits on arid, parched land in the southwestern part of Arizona where the desert temperature reaches 130°F in the shade, and dust storms whip up $50,000 worth of damage to buildings. In winters, the mercury drops below freezing. Poston, near a Native American reservation, became the temporary place for 20,000 Japanese Americans to live for almost four years.

Joan: You were the head librarian in Poston. Was that the community library?

Mabel: Yes. Prior to evacuation, I had been working under civil service at City Hall, the Bureau of Identification. As soon as the war started, they didn't want any more Japanese Americans in City Hall. They transferred us for a six-week temporary position, and I was sent to the citizen branch library as a librarian. They said it would be for six weeks and then we were terminated. When we went to Poston, I said I would like to set up a library. We started from scratch. We really set it up. And I developed a card system for checkout. It was a regular community library.

Joan: In the testimony that you gave before the commission (Commission on Wartime Relocation and Internment of Civilians) in 1981, you mentioned you had graduated from UCLA and that you had majored in sociology. So you could bring some of that expertise, although you probably didn't have a chance to order books.

Mabel: We never did order books.

Joan: Did you have Japanese newspapers?

Mabel: At our library, we didn't have Japanese books. People were very frightened and they were taking Japanese books and burning them. But at that time they were too fearful and everything was in English.

Joan: What is your memory of your first day arriving at Poston? You and Fred went together. Right? (Mabel and Fred were married at the time. Mabel was 25 years old.)

Mabel: [Mabel nodded]. *On the way, there was one incident. We stopped at—I think it was Barstow—for our lunch, and when we walked in, that proprietor said, 'We don't feed Japs.' So we couldn't eat our lunch. We were starved by the time we got to Poston. The soil was freshly turned over and the barracks were put on it. So the soil was very loose. There was no vegetation and every time you took a step the dust would rise. You really couldn't see across the street because the sand was so thick. I remember I just ran into the first barrack near me to keep the sand from blowing in my eyes, nose, and mouth.*

Joan: Had you ever experienced dust storms like that before?

Mabel: *Never. Never like that.*

Joan: Did the roof ever fly off or the power go off?

Mabel: *Well, we didn't have water in our building at the beginning. Later everyone planted things and we had water. Farmers started tilling the soil around us to raise vegetables. So then the dust storms weren't that severe.*

Joan: Since you were raised in Holtville—

Mabel: I was really raised in Calexico (a town near Holtville in Imperial Valley).

Early Years: Calexico to Los Angeles

Mabel Ota related to me how she got her name, Mabel. "When my father took me to kindergarten at age five, on my first day of school, the teacher asked my name. I replied 'Tokako Kawashima.' The teacher exclaimed that that's too difficult for the students to pronounce. 'What is an American name we can use?' she asked. My father responded, 'I always like how the maple trees in Japan turned a flaming red. What about Maple?' he asked. The teacher corrected, 'Oh, you mean Mabel. That's what we'll call her.'"

Mabel Ota avowed, "I always hated my name and would have much preferred Maple. The children when they jumped rope chanted, 'Mabel, Mabel, set the table.'"

Her home in Los Angeles is graced with classical and modern Japanese art. Plaques honoring her late husband, Fred, and herself are clustered together in the room in which Madeline does her needlework. Spunky, T.J. and Coby, her dogs, also share her home (now only one dog, T.J. is there).

Returning to our oral history interview, Mabel Ota continued:

Mabel: *I graduated from Calexico High School and went directly to UCLA. In 1940, Mabel Ota helped to organize Japan Night in El Centro. [At Camp] I was busy setting up the library. My husband was the community enterprise director. I was in Block 6 and my parents were in the block across the street. And then, of course, I got pregnant.*

Front row, L-R: Mabel Kawashima's sister Margaret, Mabel
Back row, L-R: Mabel's mother-Iyo and father-Suozo, San Diego, California, 1920-21.

Mabel Kawashima in front of Royce Hall, UCLA, 1935.

Mabel Kawashima Ota's husband Fred and Mabel, Poston, Arizona, Block 5, May, 1944 after they returned to camp from New York City.

Joan: Would you say that Japanese culture continued?

Mabel: Yes. Like my father, they would collect the dry hot ironwood and I have a number of vases that he made. My mother went to classes where she carved little tiny birds and painted them and made pins. [Vases and pins like those are on exhibit at the national exhibit "A More Perfect Union" at the Smithsonian.]

Stories Handed Down

Joan: Do you remember any stories that your mother and father told you that you passed on to your daughters?

Mabel: When we were small, there weren't many Japanese in the city, only a handful of families. We did get teased by others and sometimes we'd get angry and they would say things like 'Chin, Chin, [Chin----].' I would come home and tell my parents and my father said, 'You know you are a descendent of a Samurai, *so be proud. Be very proud of your heritage. And you can hold your head up high.'*

Joan: That's an important story.

Mabel: I always remembered that. Don't give up and really strive. I have said that to my daughters.

Joan: Do you think Japanese cultural values became stronger in camp or less strong?

Mabel: I think cultural values weakened.

Joan: Did you ever notice if Japanese American women communicated the same way in camp as they did outside of camp?

Mabel: On our block [in camp] those who volunteered were outspoken types. We always communicated.

Joan: There were many Japanese Americans together (in camp). In that sense that might be different from the context in which you grew up, and at UCLA. Probably at that time there were not 41percent or even 30 percent Asian Americans attending UCLA.

Mabel: When I went to UCLA in 1934, there were very few of us. Most Japanese felt that their sons should go but they didn't think their daughters needed college. 'How come you went to college?' my friends would ask me. 'We didn't go to college,' they would say. 'Our parents sent us to Japan for a year.' But in our family, since we didn't have any sons, I always said, 'I'm going to college,' and it was just understood when I graduated I could go to college.

Joan: Were you the older?

Mabel: Yes. When I went to college here I left a town of about 12,000 people and UCLA had 20,000 students. The Japanese American women students were not allowed to join sororities or live in the dorms. So I spent my first year in Boyle Heights at the Japanese YWCA. The dean of women at UCLA organized Kai Alpha Delta sorority, a Japanese American sorority. It was organized in 1928 so we would have a group to relate to, and enjoy the affiliate activities. I was very fortunate.

I said to my Big Sister, Frances, who was a senior, I said, 'I want to major in education because I always wanted to be a teacher.' She said, 'Mabel, that's what I wanted to be but the dean told us there's no use in being an education major because you won't ever get a job.' At that time, that was very true. There wasn't a single Asian teacher in California.

Joan: What was most difficult in camp during the first period of time that you were there?

Mabel: It was a shocking experience to arrive there and step into all that dust. We had to fill our mattresses with hay and bring it back and put it on there [steel-spring army cots]. I always think of hay being soft in the movies, but it was really hard. I always remember that.

Joan: With the cracks in the floor, there must have been creatures that got in.

Mabel: That's right. At that time, it was mostly dust. Every time there was a dust storm, all the dust would come in and we connected a hose to the outside faucet and we'd wash all the dust off.

Joan: Hose it down. After you got pregnant, what was your most difficult time?

Mabel: Well, it was what happened at birth.

Heartbreaks

Mabel Kawashima Ota testified at the 1981 Hearings about the birth of Madeline.[1] In her words, "There was only one O.B. doctor for the entire camp. I had long, long hours of labor…28 hours of labor. The nurses finally sent for the doctor. I must have looked ghastly… My sister left the room abruptly (to go outside to vomit)." The doctor told Mabel that her baby's heartbeat was getting very faint and that forceps would have to be used. She would be given a local because there was no anesthesiologist. She remembered the delivery room. "I thought the forceps looked like ice tongs used by the ice man when he delivered a block of ice. After much pulling, he finally got the baby out. She gave a faint cry. She was rushed to the incubator and I didn't see her for three days. When I saw her, I noticed a large scab on the back of her head. Madeline is a developmentally disabled person. She is mentally retarded and has grand mal epilepsy."[2]

Joan: Fred, your husband, had gotten a job in New York City at this time, so you were alone, giving birth to your baby, Madeline. You didn't have the emotional support of Fred.

Mabel: Because of her and her problems—Madeline—it really changed my life. When we came back to Los Angeles [after camp], my pediatrician said, 'Mabel, you need to take her to Children's Hospital and have Dr. Little's opinion; really have her examined.' Dr. Little was the head of the hospital. She had all these different tests and Dr. Little said, 'There was evidence of brain damage and her development will depend entirely on the type of education you expose her to.'

Turning Points

Joan: What a jolt! A turning point in your life.

Mabel: Yes. I was really shocked. I came home and thought about it and talked to my husband about it and said, 'You know, I don't know what elementary education or secondary education is, so I need to go back to school.' And he agreed. I went back to California State, Los Angeles, and went there in the spring semester and took the required classes. I had already graduated from University of California at Los Angeles. Then during the summer, I did my practice teaching. At about this time, my younger daughter, Candice, was born. And then I read in the newspaper that a Japanese American teacher had been hired by the Los Angeles City School District because there was a shortage of teachers. I said, 'My, I think I'll try for it.' At the end of my practice teaching I took the city exam and I got a telegram within a week: 'You're hired.'

Joan: Do you recall what year that was?

Mabel: September 1949. I was the second or third Japanese American to be hired.

Joan: When you were in camp, did you surmise that anything was wrong with Madeline?

Mabel: Yes. In the same barracks, another lady was pregnant also. She gave birth to a little girl the same week I gave birth to Madeline one month in early April. We made comparisons. Her child was more animated and she could roll over and sit up—and Madeline—she didn't walk until she was 22 months. So all along, I said, 'She is very slow and it must be because of the damage because of what happened at birth.'

I didn't see her for the first three days after birth because they said she's too weak to be moved. When I did see her, she had that scar and there's a spot [on her head] where her hair has never grown.

Joan: It must have been very difficult to take care of her. Were you able to get milk for her as an infant?

Mabel: At first I breast fed her but I didn't think I had very much milk, so then, yes, they did provide it.

Joan: For some months that was an issue at camp, that they didn't get milk. The milk policy was an issue I have heard.

Mabel: We got powdered milk for the babies.

Joan: And were you able to get soap to wash the baby's clothes? The Cornell Archives papers said that that also was an issue. That they had rationed soap.

Mabel: I don't remember a shortage of soap at that time. I wanted to join my husband [in New York City]. She [Madeline] was too weak to leave camp so I waited until the doctors said she was strong enough. We left in November for New York.

Joan: From what I understand in your testimony (National Archives) your mother asked you to return to camp.

Mabel: Yes. My father was very ill. He had diabetes. In Holtville, we were able to control his diet. But in camp, there were no special diets. Sometimes the diet would be completely different starches, especially at the beginning. Until we raised our own vegetables, we didn't have fresh vegetables.[3]

Joan: There seemed to be a food deprivation for babies, the elderly, pregnant women and those with special conditions.

Joan: When you went to New York City from Poston to join Fred, your husband, how was that trip for you?

Mabel: I managed. It was a new experience. It was very cold. Really cold [November]. We lived on Claremont Avenue across from the International House [near Columbia University]. We lived on the fourth floor. The apartment was very cold. We had to wash our laundry in a tub in the kitchen near the stove. And then hang the laundry in the kitchen.

Madeline Ota, Los Angeles, CA, 1946, after camp.

Joan: When you had to go back to camp five months later how did you feel?

Mabel: It was important to go back because my mother was alone. We didn't intend to stay there for very long.

Joan: And then the circumstance with your father—

Mabel: That was real tragic because after we went back, the camp told us that the doctor misdiagnosed him. They said he had melancholy, but we had no way of treating him but we could send him to the Phoenix Rest Home where he could have treatment.

Joan: He suffered electric shock therapy there.

Mabel: And he went through that, but then he passed away; soon after, the physician there said that he had been misdiagnosed and he really died from diabetes, in a diabetic coma.

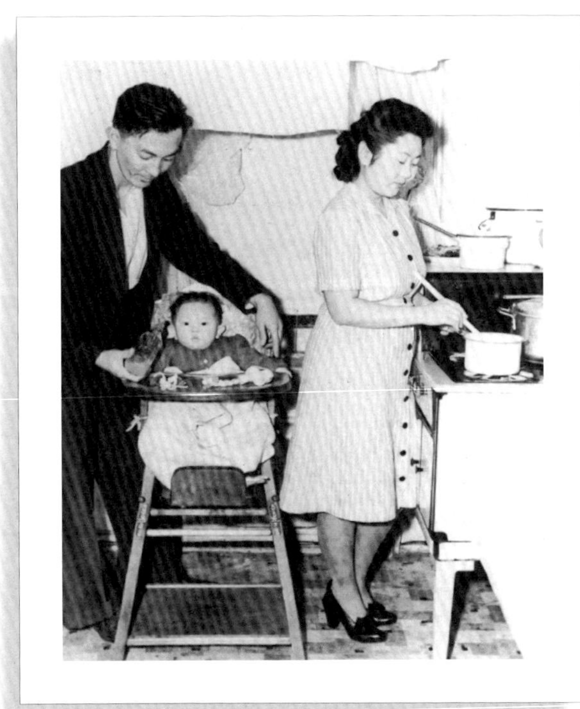

Fred K. Ota, baby Madeline Ota and Mabel Kawashima Ota, New York City apartment about December 1943. Wet laundry is hung on a metal rack and then raised overhead to act as a clothesline.

Joan: That's reprehensible. After the death of your father, you decided to go to Denver.

Mabel: Well, Fred had a friend who had opened a soy sauce shop. He needed help. He offered Fred a job.

Joan: You were in Denver and then you moved to California. How was that decision made?

Mabel: We always said we were going back. After all, our home was still there.

Joan: The reason I asked about it is, from my reading, I understand that people were told they shouldn't go back to California; in fact, there was a move against Japanese Americans returning to the West Coast. I think the few families who returned were courageous, knowing that there might be a backlash and discrimination.

New Frontiers

Mabel: To tell the truth, I never even thought about that. One of your questions was at what point in your life did you move beyond the camp experience. When I took that teacher's exam and was immediately hired it gave me a lift. Saying, I can achieve as well as anyone else.

Joan: It was another turning point, then. And that you transcended those two tragedies that had happened.

Mabel: One of my pupils said, 'Mrs. Ota, you should become an administrator.' I hadn't even thought of that, but when she said 'you should really go back and get a master's degree and become an administrator,' I gave it a thought. I said, 'That's what I'm going to do.'

Joan: So you did that?

Mabel: Yes. I did. I became a principal. I was the first Asian teacher consultant for the city. In 1962 I was the first Asian woman principal in California.

Joan: What an achievement!

Mabel: After I retired I have been very active in my community. I belong to the Los Angeles Executive Board, the Los Angeles City Council on Aging. Also, the Executive Board of the Asian Pacific Coalition for Aging, the Board of the Senior Citizen Center, and chaired the Legislative Advocacy Council. My greatest achievement since retirement is when I went to the Seinan Senior Citizen Center to take cultural classes and take calligraphy. [She has also taken classes in such areas as Ikebana, *Japanese History and Culture and Line Dancing.]*

Joan: Something for *you.* When did you retire?

Mabel: 1980. The director [at the center] said, 'We need someone to go to these senior meetings. So won't you go, since you're bilingual?' The first meeting I attended was at USC [University of Southern California.] It was a southern California seniors group having a meeting to come up with issues to discuss at a State House Conference on Aging in Sacramento, and I went. I was directed to the legal legislation committee. I found out that seniors had many needs. Each committee was supposed to select a representative to that State House Conference. I got elected. I went to Sacramento for that conference. After that, I ran for senior assemblywoman, representing Los Angeles and I won. I went there in 1983 and was elected again. After two terms, I said, 'I think I will concentrate on local groups.'

Joan: I had a chance to reread the testimony that you gave in 1981 (for the hearings on the Japanese American Internment, held in various cities in the United States). I remember your saying (to me) that it was one of the most difficult things you ever had to do. How did you come to make the decision to testify?

Mabel: The JACL [Japanese American Citizen League] president said, 'Mabel, you went to Poston, so why won't you testify?' I said, 'I don't want to testify, but I'm willing to write my testimony.' I wrote my story and he read it. And he said, 'You know, Mabel, you should really testify orally before the committee.' I did want my story to be known because we certainly don't want this type of thing ever to happen again, so that's why I testified. When I testified, all my emotions came out. It was really difficult because it brought back all those memories, the hurt and discrimination. It was really hard.

Joan: Were there many people in the audience?

Mabel: *It was completely full, the auditorium.*

Joan: It was a large group then.

Mabel: *Yes. It was very difficult.*

Joan: As you look back on your life, what are the important things or values that you want your daughters (Candice and Madeline) to remember about you?

Mabel: *You have the spirit of the* Samurai *and you should be proud and really strive. If you don't try, you won't achieve. Don't ever give up and you'll be successful.*

Joan: You were saying that the Disability Act passed several years ago.

Mabel: *That was around November of '92. So Madeline has been attending the ECF [Exceptional Children's Art Center] every day. I served six years on the board of the regional center for developmentally disabled in Los Angeles. Then I was appointed by the mayor to serve on the Commission for the Disabled.*

Joan: You have not only raised your daughter, Madeline, but you have given back to the community where you can contribute; you have really brought about social change.

Mabel: *Yes. And so with this tape [videotape on developmentally disabled] I hope that she's [Madeline is] going to show it in Japan. I guess Japan is interested in improving their program for the disabled.*

Joan: You're really on the frontier, forging ahead, in areas that are not yet laid down, especially in Japan. You really act as a role model.

Mabel: *I keep very active. Because I was a senior assemblywoman, I met many of the California legislators. One was Senator Daramendi. The California senior legislators asked him to propose legislation and all of us worked very hard to get it through the legislature. It was an initiative which was put on the ballot in the following November so that the people in California would have a chance to vote on this Senior Center Bond Act. We worked again. It passed.*

Joan: What an accomplishment!

Mabel: *Each city received funds for senior centers. The seniors were notified to write a proposal for a grant. I went to the director and said we need to write a grant for this proposal and submit it, which was done and our center received funding.*

Mabel Kawashima Ota measured her life using as a watermark, these words: "If I can get through camp and what it dealt me, I can get through anything." Threading her way through arduous hurdles, Kawashima Ota encountered several pivotal events in her life. These life-changing events are bookmarks in her life.

Mabel Kawashima Ota and husband, Fred. Poston Reunion, Los Angeles, CA. December, 1995.

Fred Ota, daughter Madeline and Mabel, Luminaries Restaurant, Los Angeles. August 14, 1993.

L-R: Mabel Ota, daughter Candy Funakoshi, sister Margaret Iwashita on Mabel Ota's eighty-eighth birthday, 2004.

(Right to Left) Mabel, Fred, daughter Candice Funakoshi, son-in-law Gary Funakoshi, Grandson Keith Funakoshi, Grandson Brent Funakoshi, daughter Madeline. June 16, 1996. Westwood, CA.

The birth of Madeline and the slow, imperceptible surmise of a misdiagnosis through comparison with other babies made Mabel Kawashima Ota wonder what the problem might be. Madeline had suffered brain damage at birth and would need special education for the rest of her life. The discovery sent shockwaves through Kawashima Ota and even today her concerns remain that after she dies what will become of Madeline?* During this period Kawashima Ota's father misdiagnosed with melancholia suffered electroshock treatments for a condition he did not have. Medical tests later proved that her father had diabetes which resulted in a diabetic coma and death. This appalling bungling was yet another irreversible tragic outcome of the internment.

Kawashima Ota's response to her child's problems led to her decision to become certified in education to help teach Madeline and fulfill her own career goals.

Realizing that she could advance professionally, she pursued a master's degree in educational administration which led to an appointment as the first Asian American principal in California. Continuously she has translated adversity into opportunities to serve others, as she did by establishing the library in Poston, setting the precedents in California education, becoming a senior assemblywoman and passing legislation for the Senior Center Bond Act—all, while placing her first priority on her daughters. Madeline attends and participates in a workshop making handicrafts. Candice works in library administration at the University of California at San Diego.

Like the purple morning glory seeds that Mabel Kawashima Ota had taken to camp and planted, her life unfolded and bloomed with hope and optimism. Her transcendent spirit, like the purple morning glories, still remains.

*Madeline Ota passed away August 4, 2005.

Only at desert camp
barrack doors do they bloom
purple morning glories

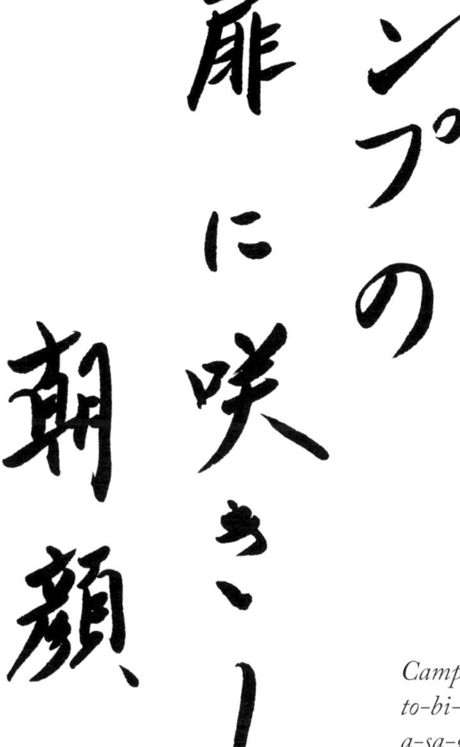

Camp no
to-bi-ra ni sa-ki-shi
a-sa-ga-o yo

Mary Shigematsu's family. L-R Mother, Mitsuye Shigematsu, siblings Kerrie, Hideko, Min, Joe, Marie, Mary; Father Mosaku Shigematsu in second row.

Chapter 2

IN MARY SHIGEMATSU HOSHIZAKI'S OWN WORDS

Another Imperial Valley girl who grew up in the valley was Mary Shigematsu Hoshizaki. Resolute and self-reliant, she handled hardship and camp and moved on becoming active in the Japanese American Citizen League of Imperial Valley. This is her story.

Before Camp

Joan: What was life like before camp?

Mary: *I attended Japanese school and learned the cultural traditions of flower arrangement and tea ceremony. I graduated from Central High in El Centro. Then I attended Woodbury College in Los Angeles where I studied design of clothing and hats. The major was called Costume Arts and Illustration. My mother's advice was, 'Women should know how to sew to become a homemaker.' That's why I went to school. I graduated from college and then I got married to George. We had a pool hall and soda fountain.*

Joan: How long were you married before camp?

Mary: *Three years. I entered camp in 1942.*

Joan: Did you measure your life by the yardstick of the camp?

Mary: *My life was tough before camp. My husband had a partnership business and the partner stole everything.*

Mary Shigmatsu, high school graduation, El Centro, CA.

Then Came Poston

Mary Shigematsu Hoshizaki tells her story upon arrival at camp.

Mary: *My infant daughter cried all night that first day we arrived at camp. No one would open the mess hall for milk. I had milk in a thermos but it had spoiled, so I asked if I could have some milk for my baby.*

Joan: How old were you when you entered camp?

Mary: *I was about twenty-five. My oldest daughter was one and a half years old and Carolyn was eight months old. I had a son born in camp. He was a month old when we came out.*

Joan: How did you arrange to get milk for your baby?

Mary: *The next day the mess hall was open and we got milk.*

Mary Shigematsu Hoshizaki in wedding kimono, El Centro, CA.

Although she was able to get milk that next day, milk continued to be a critical concern for infants, the young, and pregnant nursing mothers. Women formed block women's and mother's clubs, and public health was one of their issues. A number of meetings were devoted to formulating policy on who got the milk. On June 11, 1942, the Mother's Club raised the issue of canned milk versus fresh milk. Dr. A. H. Leighton, Chief of the Public Health Department, Lt. Commander, Medical Corps, United States Naval Reserves, addressed the women on July 16, 1942, and related his views. He thought the canned milk should be used for babies up to the age of one and one-half years, although if mothers wanted to use fresh milk, they should be able to; that children one and one-half to six should have all the milk they wanted; then older children and sick adults. Then different plans in different blocks were reported. Next, Leighton asked the members of the club to discuss what they wanted to do, and report back in a week. The following questions were raised:

1. Can we assume that all children under one and a half years will take canned milk?
2. That those between one and a half and six should have the first chance?
3. That those between six and ten should be the next group?
4. That some should be kept for sick people?
5. That any left over should be used for anyone?
6. What about expectant and nursing mothers?

Other issues were discussed at the meeting, such as "cooking utensils and danger of mixing salads in metal pans."[1]

On July 18, 1942, a joint meeting of the Women's Club and the Mother's Club was held to again discuss the milk policies and a plan formulated. The women were told that powdered milk was unnecessary with the abundance of canned milk. The tentative plan included that first choice would be one and a half to six years; second choice would be six to ten years; third choice-invalids; fourth choice-nursing and pregnant expectant mothers. Questions were raised about the older children (ten to sixteen years). Would they be given any milk? Women were informed that if there were to be any milk left over after the needs groups, the older children would probably get their share.[2]

Mary Shigematsu Hoshizaki and baby Wayne.

"When the milk supply was cut, some blamed the women for meddling and causing the shortage, although they had only been informed that the shortage would occur and asked to work out the best possible method of distribution for what milk there would be."[3] Another issue in addition to milk deprivation was food shortages that women protested. There was the practice of not feeding lunch to the seasonal workers. The leader of the Women's Club was Ms. Findley whose goals were "a means of communication." She encouraged the women to step out of their traditional roles and to take part in community life. Through her encouragement several women ran for the Temporary Community Council, and one was elected.[4] Through these clubs, women had a voice and influence on important issues. The club became a channel for the women to form a PTA, to discuss problems of children having too much freedom and not eating together as a family, and use their influence with the administration on everything from availability of fresh vegetables, milk shortage, heat prostration, sex education, contagious disease, nursery school, sun stroke, finding teachers, and building schools.[5] One telling notation is a statement that on the first anniversary meeting, July 16, 1943, every European American head had been sent an invitation; only three showed up.[6]

As we can see, milk was monitored very closely.

Joan: Were there any support groups?

Mary: No. In one room we were four adults and three children, so there were seven in one room. There was no privacy. Eventually we would get a charcoal stove with two burners and food from the outside because George drove a truck to Parker (small nearby town) to pick up supplies.

Joan: Were there many hardships? You mentioned you had two children when you entered camp.

Mary: Marilyn was one and a half; Carolyn was eight months, and Wayne was born in camp.

Joan: Did you have any problems with the pregnancy or birth?

Mary: None, but there were no vitamins, calcium supplements, or fresh fruits and vegetables for pregnant women.

Joan: Do you think there was more communication in camp with your friends or parents?

Mary: I didn't participate in anything. I didn't go out much. I spoke Japanese to my parents. I did have one good friend, though. But she didn't have children and I felt isolated.

Joan: What were the biggest obstacles in camp?

Mary: Lack of privacy. My husband George and I, my two small children, and my best friend shared the barrack. There was only a sheet which divided the two families. There were seven in our barrack. We had mutton all the time, the same. My husband wouldn't eat lamb. At the latrine, there was no privacy. We were in Block 60. There were more older people and farmers. The dust storms were monstrous.

Mary Shigematsu Hoshizaki at Poston in front of recreation hall. Back row, first from left.

Many people who were at Poston talk about the dust storms. Henry Sigura comments in his journal about how bitter people were "against the builders for putting up such flimsy structures. Many said they got under their beds for safety when the roofs began cracking and ripping off. The power was out and candles were used."[7]

Elmer Tanigoshi writes, "The power lines down. The wind and dust increased until the surrounding landscape was almost entirely obscured from vision." People were "badly shaken. Many people went to bed feeling faint and weak from their terrible experience." Every time Tanigoshi saw dark, low, heavy-hanging rain clouds approaching across the top of the mesquite brush which bordered his block, he wondered if the storm would be another tornado-like force which laid the block in ruin. Cyclone cellars had been dug to provide shelter from such storms, as well as relief from the heat.[8]

Yoshiko Kubo wrote: "The mad rush, people running from every which way into their apartments to close windows. The rain at 8:30 p.m. was pouring down at a forty-degree angle, whipped by the wind. Lightning raced across the sky, almost resembled a cat's paw in the set of snatching its prey. Sister Ruth began crocheting to take her mind off the lightning which frightened her. George and I looked at each other and smirked. Crocheting in the dark… that's how frightened she was."[9]

After the storm, Kubo writes: "Rain had poured into this apartment. T'was like living outdoors."[10] F.M. describes Block 2: roofs were blown to all parts of the block. Telephone lines and wires were cut off. Lumber was lying all around. Windows in the women's latrines were broken. Loose electric wires were all over the ground.[11] F.M. continues: "Last evening along 7:30, my sister and I were watching the baseball game on field #30 between the Golden Bears [Los Angeles] and Valley [Brawley] teams. We had settled ourselves comfortably on canvas camping chairs right by the catcher's plate as we were told that this was one of the good games. The first inning went by with a whizz-bang! Three outs in a row. As we sat quietly, our spirits not yet aroused, I noticed in a distance from the same direction of our last storm, a cloud of dust heading in our direction. We stayed to the last minute. It struck us much sooner than we had anticipated and we made a dash for home. Just in time."[12]

Seizo Sakamoto observes about the storm that people can endure hardship if they have hope for a better future. Further, that people are apt to relish their capacity of "endurance in hardship" and will forget what they suffered in the past.[13]

Another observer commented, "Most Japanese will take what they consider an act of God very calmly; but they do not take easily an act of the government which they consider unfair. The windstorm was an act of God—but the roofs flying off the houses was an act of the government. The government should have seen to it that the roofs were put on to stay."[14]

Mary continued: *My husband, George, worked in construction driving a truck and worked in the camouflage [nets used in the war] plant. Then my husband went to Utah to work while I stayed in camp and took care of three small children. I had two brothers and three sisters. My brother, Joe, went into the Army Language School and worked for the Military Intelligence in Japan. My brother, Minoru, was in the 442nd.*

The 442nd Regimental Combat Team was a U.S. Army regiment made up of Nisei who saw heavy action during World War II. The 442nd suffered the highest casualty rate and was the most decorated unit for its size and length of service in American military history.[15] Moreover, they helped to liberate Dachau.[16] The contradictions between the internment betrayal and the heroism of Shigematsu Hoshizaki's brothers and thousands of others provide one of the supreme ironies of the war.

After Camp: Discrimination and Challenges

Mary: *My husband, George, worked in Utah but he came back to camp and we left for El Centro together. When we came out of camp, we had nothing. We stayed in a vacant building. With three kids, no one wanted to rent to us.*

Joan: And your husband?

Mary: *After camp, he had one leg amputated and then later, he had to have the other amputated. He was a double amputee. He died a year ago.*

Joan: I'm sorry to hear that. What happened to your pool hall and soda fountain? Who watched over it?

Mary: *[European American] friends watched over it. It was returned to us but most Japanese American people had left the valley so a lot of people weren't playing pool. There was a lot of discrimination.*

Joan: You had a lot of courage to return to El Centro. After you gave up the pool hall, how did you manage?

Mary: *We did farming on a small scale with friends. Then we went off on our own. We stayed in farming until there was a labor problem and then we gave it up. Then I got a job with an insurance agency, Pan American Underwriters Insurance Agency.*

Joan: What were the turning points in your life?

Mary: *Camp; having children, college; and my job as a claims adjuster in El Centro. I worked there for sixteen years. I even wore pants.*

Joan: What would you suggest to be done in the U.S. so that this (camp) doesn't happen again?

Mary: Educate people. Just because we have the face of an Asian, doesn't mean we are bad. After all, we are citizens, too. One of my brothers was in the 442nd in Italy during the war. People are still prejudiced.

Jason Jackson

Mary Shigematsu Hoshizaki, winner of deep sea fishing competition in San Diego, 1997.

Briefly then, we have seen that milk and food were only two of the many deprivations which people had to endure in camp. Clean and hot water, heat, cooling systems, privacy, amenities of home, cars, telephones, washing machines, freedom to travel, to protest, and lack of educational motivation were only a partial list of the deprivations. Moreover, the dust storms permeated everything.

Although Mary Shigematsu Hoshizaki's remembrances are painful, she moved on in her life. A strong woman before camp, she found even more strength within herself in and beyond camp. Perhaps these hardships that Mary Shigematsu Hoshizaki lived through before camp helped to prepare her in part to deal with camp, and post camp shock.

Confronting discrimination was difficult, Mary Shigematsu Hoshizaki recollects: "When we came out of camp with our three children, no one wanted to rent to us." Shigematsu Hoshizaki wants people to learn and remember those difficult times.

Breaking New Ground

One of her great stress relievers was fishing. It became her passion! Her grandson, Jason Jackson, recalls that his grandfather, George, at first wouldn't take Mary fishing because he thought she would get seasick.[17] To his surprise, she didn't and loved it. She in fact became the first woman to not only break the male barrier in salt-water fishing in San Diego but to catch a yellow tail in a derby and to win a car. An astute negotiator, Mary traded her car, since she already had one, for an air conditioning system for her home. Both Mary and George became well known at the San Diego Fisherman's Landing. "Mary outfished the men," Jason concluded.

To honor the memory of Japanese American families, the Japanese American Gallery in the Imperial County Historical Society Pioneers' Museum was founded in Imperial, California and Mary Shigematsu Hoshizaki spoke at the opening ceremonies. She, as an Imperial Valley Nisei woman, gave assurances their legacy would continue. Lastly, it needs to be said that Mary Shigematsu Hoshizaki was active in the Japanese American community and served as Treasurer of the Japanese American Citizens League, Imperial Valley Chapter.

Joan Loveridge-Sanbonmatsu

Mary Shigematsu Hoshizaki's grandson Jason Jackson, President, Japanese American Citizens League, Imperial Valley Chapter, welcoming folks at the Operation Recognition Ceremonies and Banquet, April 29, 2005. The torch has been passed.

L-R Mary Shigematsu Hoshizaki's husband George, grandson Jason Jackson, Mary, grandson Randy Rice, 1988.

Jason Jackson

Mary Shigematsu Hoshizaki and Alaskan Malamute dog, Kuma, 2000.

Jason Jackson

Mary Shigematsu Hoshizaki showing sushi, Arigato Sushi Bar, El Centro, CA 2000.

"Plant the seed of positiveness and empower people."

Chapter 3

MARY MITAMURA SANBONMATSU'S NARRATIVE

"Just look at the positive," explained Mary Mitamura as she emphasizes a primary value. By internment she had been dealt a negative situation. Not only did Mary Mitamura Sanbonmatsu develop a sense of humor but she also developed a positive philosophy toward life which sustains her today. She declares, "I don't think it has anything to do with age" (the youngest—a teenager in camp—of the five women interviewed). "Plant the seed of positiveness and empower people. I want people to be strong and independent." Today, she sees herself as a troubleshooter, very practical, and believes that you have to "stick to the core in the line of thinking."

Education at Camp

Educational motivation in 1942, however, was difficult to muster. It was not the stone skimming across the river creating small ripples, then larger ripples, nor the snowball rolling down a snow-covered hill, gathering snow, energy, and speed as it moved faster and faster. Education at camp was an obstacle course. The schools had to be built, adobe brick by adobe brick which were laid mostly by women.[1] Fifteen years old and in high school at the time, Mary Mitamura remembers making her own table and chair and dragging them across the compound from one class to another, if she wanted something to sit on. The classes were scheduled so that one class would be on one end of the compound and classes for the college track curriculum would be at the other end, two miles away. It was impossible to get there on time, she concluded.

The Director of Guidance, Miss Cushman, reported on school problems: "We have had at least 350 changes in the schedule by the high school students up until now, in one week's time (October 5—October 12, 1942). You can hardly blame them when they find that they have chemistry in one block and then have to walk a mile to their typing class and another mile back to their core class."[2]

There were horrendous delays with the textbook orders. The textbooks ordered for fall came after Christmas. Children sat on apple crates. Classes were held in freezing low temperatures. Often teachers took the pupils with their coats on outside to stand around a campfire until the middle of the morning. Stoves arrived in January and proved to be inadequate to heat the barracks properly.[3]

Mary Mitamura Sanbonmatsu recalls that there were no books, pencils or crayons in camp. Everything was on ditto or mimeographed sheets. Before camp, the schools in Imperial had books and everything. The Mitamura family even had a typewriter in their home, unlike camp.

Camp

Mary: *They didn't have tables, or chairs, or books, or anything [in camp], so we made them, printed copies and printed books. They weren't books, just pamphlets. We had to carry everything, whatever we made. If we made a chair and a table, we carried it from block to block.*

Joan: Wasn't it awfully hot to do that?

Mary: *Oh yes. But when you're that age you just do as you're told. I was a junior and senior while I was in Poston. Sometimes you got discouraged with so much walking because you would have to watch because you may have a course here, and you may have to be at the other end in ten minutes. You could never make it in time.*

Joan: If you're late, they would probably think there is no good reason, whereas, in fact, it was a very long, long walk. I wonder if some students took easier courses so they wouldn't have to make the long walk.

Mary: *I guarantee that. It did not do any of us any good as far as school went. Until we went to camp my parents were always after us about education. When we went to camp we had to study from these little sheets of paper instead of a book. It didn't exactly make us feel gung-ho about school and really getting into college. You went day by day. We were living sort of suspended. We had no ambition.*

Bare schools gave the students an empty feeling: no books, no chairs, no desks, no blackboards, no central school building, no adequate heat or cooling systems.

(L-R) Back row, fourth. Mary Mitamura. Lantana School, 1939.

Mary Mitamura dragging her chair across the compound to class at Poston. Age 17.

In May, 30 coolers were ordered, but 200 were needed to handle 120° daily heat. Students and teachers asked why the administrative offices "are adequately provided with coolers and we have to endure the heat?"[4]

"The older children in most cases, apparently were too bewildered and embittered to provide themselves with improvised seats. They sat on or lolled over tables until the chairs, purchased on the outside, arrived."[5]

The students had been evacuated from schools that were the best in the country. "Children longed for their former homes, schools and schoolmates. The youths were bewildered by the fact that they had been treated as enemy aliens even though they were American citizens." In the "Work Experience Unit" of the curriculum, the wages per hour were seven cents.[6]

Although one hundred and eleven teachers were Japanese American, eighty-nine were European American; many teachers had not been trained as teachers. In fact, thirty five per cent were college graduates, while the remainder had only two to three years of college work to their credit and there were sixty children in some classes, including first grade.[7]

Mary Mitamura, age 14. Before Poston.

A number of students wrote about their apathetic attitude; students like Ted Kato. He asked if something couldn't be done about the school environment to help his lethargic attitude.[8]

In the Poston Senior High School Curriculum Bulletin (1943-1944), six study plans were printed for students to follow: agriculture, bookkeeping, college preparatory, homemaking, shop, and stenographic. In four out of the six, work experience is urged. The only two which don't have work experience included were "college prep" and "homemaking." Further, "it is recommended that college preparatory students carry an additional elective each year in order that they shall be able to acquire vocational skills in addition to college entrance credits during their high school course."[9] It was incumbent upon the college preparatory student to seek out a core teacher to check on specific requirements for certain fields.

In a report "Guidance and Evaluation in the Poston Schools, 1942-1943," the Director of Guidance, Frances S. Cushman stated, "We [teachers] cannot say, 'Here is the school best suited to your needs,' but rather the question must be 'to what school can you go?'" Students were counseled not to prepare for college entrance requirements for a particular college, "but rather that they must prepare so that they can take advantage of the opportunity that comes." In addition, teachers advised students to take "one or more vocational skills in case they do not realize their ambitions of going to college."[10]

The lowering of standards appears to be telling the student not to aim high, because the guidance counselor doesn't think he or she will get into the college of choice. Moreover, the second message is to be sure to have fallback vocational skills in case one doesn't get into college.

This prejudicial attitude is further reflected in the Personal and Family Information form which each student completed.[11] Nowhere on the form does it ask the student about educational goals. It does, however, ask about vocational plans. There are no questions about postgraduate schooling or college.

Mary Mitamura Sanbonmatsu continues her narrative about her teenage years in camp.

Mary: *I used to love to write plays, and stories and poems—things like that. I really enjoyed it and that's the way I was, but when I went into camp, people thought that anyone who did those kinds of things wasn't, what would you say—in the crowd. You're an oddity, so I learned fast to not do it, so I quit. I remember the English teacher...encouraging me to get back to doing that because she was always picking on me to give a speech and so on, but I just kept fouling it up, on purpose sort of, because I didn't want to be different. I wanted to be one of the crowd, and blend in.*

Joan: When you entered camp at age fifteen—did you and others know it was going to be for three and one half years?

Mary: *No. They just picked us up and took us and you just stayed there until... well when they finally let us out.*

Joan: You were involved in sports in high school?

Mary: *We played mainly softball and basketball.*

Joan: There were girls' clubs. Were you a member?

Mary: *No. I never got involved in clubs. Never really went to any definite church there. We were in block 39. All I remember is staying pretty close to our block. I guess maybe our parents didn't want us running around too much.*

Basketball team at Poston
L-R, standing: Ruth Kodama, Teri Ishimaru, Kazuko Nakamura, Shigeko Matsuno and Shizuko Seki, third person from end Lily Horibe; second from end Tamiko (Tanki) Kodama; Far right: Mary Mitamura. Kneeling, L-R: Harry Kodama, Sho Horibe.

A Teenager's Lighter Moments

Joan: In Poston I, the whole group—(nine thousand)—was all Japanese. I remember the comment you made to me, "It was party time." It was probably one of the few times in your life when you were living with as many as (nine thousand) Japanese and Japanese American people.

Mary: Yes. A party would be in the next block or some close by block, people that we knew in Imperial Valley—like block 26 or block 42 or block 52. Each block had their party going at least once a week.

Joan: With dances?

Mary: Yes. They had dances or a group get together. I was fifteen then. When we were fourteen or fifteen, we could see a good time.

"Stormy Weather," "All the Way," and "I'll Never Forget" played on the radio and the first football game, Bulldogs versus the Wildcats, was won 7-6.[12] On September 27, 1943, the new adobe school buildings (built by students and families), opened their doors. In December, the high school auditorium was completed. "Isn't it grand?" declared the yearbook.[13] *Porter, Please,* the first theatre production opened to a full house with the Bulldog Bounce held in January. *What a Life* was the spring play, followed by *Growing Pains* and the Junior-Senior Prom, report cards, Super Senior Week and Commencement.

Mary: We were sheltered, though, still living in the family fold, but by the time you are four or five years older, your life has been disrupted. You wonder why you have to accept it. You can be bitter. We gave lots of children's parties. I did quite a bit of organizing. I loved children. I'd put on games.

Joan: Before the war, were you involved in softball or basketball?

Mary: No. Only in Phys. Ed. But I helped my father a lot. When I was thirteen or fourteen, I packed tomatoes.

Joan: So you went to Imperial High School before camp.

Mary: Imperial is a town in Imperial County, along with Holtville and El Centro. And we would march in parades in El Centro to traditional Japanese music. My father was a farmer and we grew melons and lettuce.

Joan: I've read about the dust storms at Poston. Did they scare you?

Mary: No. We used to sit in our home which was like a barrack and my sister would look at me and say, 'Oh, you look funny', because, you know, I'm getting white hair and white eyelashes and white everything. I'd laugh and say, 'You look just like that, too,' and we would sit there and giggle. [Laughter]. We would age overnight. It was funny looking at each other turning white. We had never faced dust storms like that before here, in the valley, because in the valley our homes were better. Every time we do anything, I try to look at the humorous side of it instead of the bad things, so in a way, that's what sticks to you.

Joan: That's a great way to get through life.

Mary: *Those barracks—the sand came right through, almost like you were standing outside. It was really bad.*
Joan: Do you remember if ever the roof blew off or the power went out?
Mary: *The power used to go off once in a while. I don't remember the roof.*
Joan: Well, that was lucky.

Mary Mitamura, however, saw storms as an adventure, as did a few others. On July 23, 1942, Henry Sigura "went out to look and saw in the northeast direction an immense cloud of dust coming toward us. The wind began tearing off rooftops—the noise was really fearful. I saw pieces of wood, roofing paper, and debris sailing by. Aside from my worry, I enjoyed the tempest. The fury of the storm reminded me how puny man is against the elements. The fresh earthy smell when it began to rain was really enjoyable. The lightning was magnificent." During the height of the storm, the children ran around feeling each other's hearts and shouting, "Feel my heart! Feel my heart!"[14]

Joan: Returning to the activities teenagers had in camp, I wonder about the Japanese culture—if any of the holidays were celebrated, or if the Japanese language were spoken.
Mary: *Of course, the parents were all there around us and they spoke Japanese, and the younger ones spoke to them in Japanese. In other words, just to answer questions or to do what we were told. Even with my mom or father, we never sat around and talked. Just how are you, how are things, or asked about school, just everyday things.*
Joan: Do you recall if speaking the Japanese language was disapproved of in camp? Did anyone get punished for speaking it?
Mary: *No. I think it was encouraged.*
Joan: By your parents? Was there any administrator who said it was bad to speak it?
Mary: *No.*
Joan: I guess the administration couldn't decide whether or not to make it forbidden when people first started coming to camp. It seems like they decided not to forbid it. Later on, in camp, I understand, Japanese language classes were offered.
Mary: *Yes. We all went to Japanese school but we still didn't speak Japanese. We learned only to speak to our parents.*
Joan: Before the war, were there many Japanese in your class?
Mary: *Yes. I think the kids spoke a lot of their own languages—the Chinese, Mexicans, Italians, even Germans, but for some reason the Japanese children never did. I have a feeling as if I failed because I didn't learn and I should have because they wanted me to learn. They pushed me to school and bought me books and I didn't teach Bruce [her son] much.*
Joan: When you left camp…

Mary Mitamura, age 16. Poston, 1942.

Mary: *First we went to Utah. Everybody left when they could. A lot of people like my parents stayed 'till the very end. In Utah, I helped to pack celery and peaches. As a family we picked cherries.*

Joan: How did you choose Utah?

Mary: *We had cousins living there. In camp, I worked in the district attorney's office. I worked as a waitress at the mess hall. The reason I worked in the district attorney's office was in my senior year they told me if I worked somewhere in whatever I wanted to become, I would not have to go to school after this semester. So, of course I chose to work. As I said, first we went to Utah; then I went up to San Jose and worked awhile, and then I went to Los Angeles and worked. I was living in Los Angeles and Yoshiya Sanbonmatsu [whom she met in camp] came up to see me, and we started going around and that's how come I ended up here [married and] in Holtville.*

Stories Passed On

Joan: I wonder if you remember any stories that your mother or father passed on to you.

Mary: *My mom, she would tell us things about when they moved to Arizona and then came across the desert and they had to cross rivers, get the car across and the farming here in Imperial Valley. And my father was a chef. I think I heard bits of conversation but more through my sister [Yosh].*

Joan: In camp, did you feel that some of the values like family values got stronger or less strong? Did you eat meals together?

Mary: *Yes. There was a mess hall made, and we sat at a table. Probably my folks insisted on that. We are very strong about family—always have been that way regardless of the years that go by. We are consistent that way.*

Joan: So that was important that it wasn't lost in camp. I know that some families felt it was. Did the ways of communication stay the same or change?

Mary: *Actually the same, because I was going to school before, so it was like school friends. I didn't really talk to older people very much.*

Joan: All in all, what was camp to you?

Mary: *Camp was dusty, hot and miserable, but then in the evenings there were the dances. There was my high school graduation ceremony. I learned that there were many kinds of Japanese. I had always been told that Japanese were the brightest and worked the hardest. I found out there were those who did and those who did not.*

Joan: When something is tough, do you say "I got through camp; I can get through anything?"

Mary: *I never recall even thinking about that. Camp was one of the many things that happened throughout my life. My mother and father really believed—to just do the best you can and try to accept what is. If you can't change it, you can't change it. Just look at the positive.*

Joan: So you felt that it was a continuum. It was one event in your life and that you put it behind you and just went forward.

Mary: *Exactly.*

L-R (Tanki) Tamiko Kodama and Mary Mitamura. Mary: 16 years old. Poston, 1942.

L-R Mary Mitamura Sanbonmatsu, Mary's mother, Makino Tsukiji Mitamura and cousin. Holtville, CA about 1946-1947.

Bruce Sanbonmatsu, 1987.
The next generation.

James Michael Sanbonmatsu

Mary Mitamura Sanbonmatsu playing with her dog.
Holtville, CA. April, 2005.

George Kodama

L-R Bruce Sanbonmatsu, Mary Mitamura Sanbonmatsu, Yoshiya Sanbonmatsu.
Sanbon Inc., El Centro, CA. April, 2005.

Joan: What are your thoughts about how this kind of situation can be prevented for future generations?

Mary: Through education and have positive people leading you. You have to look to the leaders and vote. You can't just sit and not say anything.

Joan: Did you have a chance to work on redress?

Mary: There were a lot of people that fought for that. We'd never get it if it weren't for the people who went out of their way to fight for it. We live a day-to-day existence and try to do the best we can to make a living. Once you have a business it seems like you acquire responsibility toward people you have around you.

Joan: It's a big responsibility because you have such a big business and so many people involved. If you look at the pattern of your success over the long road…

Mary: I always tell people there are many, many people in this world that have worked hard, and they have a lot of talent, but a lot of it is luck. You have to have luck along with everything else, in order to make it, because you could get sick, or a lot of things could happen, such as an earthquake. If you want things only your way, it's not going to work. You have to come to an understanding.

Bruce Sanbonmatsu

Yoshiya Sanbonmatsu, Mary Mitamura Sanbonmatsu, and their dogs, Sam and Duke. El Centro, November, 2005.

L-R Mary Mitamura Sanbonmatsu and Yoshiya Sanbonmatsu. Imperial Valley, 1997.

Secrets for Resiliency

Mary Mitamura has a sense of humor and seeks the positive outlook on life. In camp, she saw dust storms as an adventure. She participated in sports such as softball, and basketball, which were the centers for socializing, and provided not only fun but also a lift for the spirits. Sometimes baseball "and the anticipation of them [games] were often all that stood between sanity and despair."[15]

The *Post-Año,* the Poston High yearbook, published, in 1944, printed "Some Food for Thought". War was identified "as the greatest invention of the devil;" "the greatest mistake: giving up;" "the most expensive indulgence: hate;" "the greatest sin: fear;" "the greatest thing in all the world, bar none: love."

Mary Mitamura Sanbonmatsu has revealed then mixed feelings about camp. She remembered the dust, the misery, the lack of motivation to go to college, but she recalled the good times, too: the dances, her high school graduation, meeting Yoshiya who would later become her husband. She learned at age 15 how to develop an optimism and sense of humor which would sustain her all her life. This was her secret for resiliency.

Today, Mary Mitamura Sanbonmatsu heads jointly with Yoshiya, her spouse, and their son Bruce, President, a business named Sanbon Incorporated, a highly successful company that grows and ships produce, articulating growers in Mexico and in Imperial Valley, all over the United States. Recently, Sanbon, Inc. received an award for its community service from the Japanese American Citizens League, Imperial Valley Chapter.

Joan Loveridge-Sanbonmatsu

Sanbon Inc.

L-R: Mary Mitamura Sanbonmatsu and sister, Yosh Mitamura Kodama. Holtville, California, 1950's.

Chapter 4

YOSHIKO MITAMURA KODAMA'S LIFE HISTORY*

"There was no way I could change anything except within myself."

Yoshiko Mitamura was Mary's older sister. At age nineteen she was forced out of junior college due to the evacuation. "When World War II had started, I was in junior college. I didn't even finish one semester. I didn't feel comfortable. So I quit." Indeed, Yosh Mitamura becoming more politically aware, felt the pain of prejudice.

Early Years in Imperial Valley

Joan: What was your family life like before the war?

Yosh: We always lived in the country. My father was a traditional head of the house. He was a chef so we had a glimpse of delicacies from other cultures. He was progressive, bought books, songs, and anything he thought might help us growing up. We had a new radio—battery operated. We'd make a trip to Sears & Roebuck to exchange batteries. He bought a new typewriter. He wanted us to have it. We were among the first in the immediate neighborhood to have an iron. He took us to the movies every week. We had a car.

Yosh—one and a half to two years old.

*The reader needs to be aware that three original documents exist for this work: the oral one produced April 10, 1994; the transcription by Betty Restuccia; and the revised written documents which evolved through consultation with the interviewee, Yoshiko Mitamura Kodama. Changes from her original oral history transcript of April 10, 1994 were made by the interviewee in conference with the interviewer, Joan Loveridge-Sanbonmatsu, October 28, 1997.

Joan: What was high school like for you, before camp?

Yosh: It was a normal high school life. I went to dances, football games; our folks could not always take us so there would be friends that would come after me out in the country. Our folks had always encouraged us to continue our education.

Joan: What happened to your family right after the war had started?

Yosh: The farm—the crops were in the ground, and our father, like all the farmers, got what he could out of it, and then we worked for the person who bought it, for thirty-five cents an hour which was the going rate.

Joan: This was before you went to camp.

Yosh: There were different curfews issued [established March 24, 1942]. We could not be out after dark. We could not cross the main highway—Highway #80—to shop in El Centro because we had to go to Brawley even if it were twice as far. There were boundaries for us. [Folks had to stay within a five mile radius of their house].

Yosh Mitamura, eight or nine years old. Front row L-R, fourth from left.
Seely Grammar School, Seely, CA.

Yosh Mitamura, about age 14, and her 8th grade graduating class friends at Lantana School. 1937.

L–R, Yosh's sister Mary Mitamura, brother John Mitamura, Yosh, brother Tosh. Yosh is in 6th grade. Imperial, California.

Life As We Knew It Was Gone

Yosh: *When I first went to camp [May 22, 1942], I was very resentful. I felt at nineteen I should have had the choice to remain on the outside or be interned.*

Joan: The Poston Papers at Cornell University testify that many people agreed with you. Your life had indeed been uprooted. Did your whole family go to camp?

Yosh: *Yes. I was the oldest. Then Mary (Mitamura), my sister, and my two brothers. Leaving was disruptive; life as we knew it was gone. We were all together in one room. We were issued cot beds when we first got there. They gave us a mattress cover—which we filled with straw. We slept on that for about six months. It was during the summer. So when we got up in the morning, we got up smelling like straw. It was overwhelming. We went [to camp] in May of 1942. George Kodama and I grew up together as neighbors and schoolmates. George and I married in July 1943. There is a role for the woman. I think shortly after that, George was in and out of camp going to different jobs in a group.*

Wedding in Camp

Joan: So you were there at least three years? You had a wedding at camp?

Yosh: *In the Rec Hall. It [the ceremony] was conducted by a minister of the church, Rev. J. Kokubun.*

Joan: I read in the *Poston City Page* that your wedding was a beautiful candlelight service with about 300 guests attending.[1] Did you ever send back for any of your belongings or furniture?

Softball team at Poston. R–L, front row: end person, Yoshiko Mitamura's sister, Mary; second from end, Yoshiko Mitamura; third from end, Tamiko Kodama; fourth from end, Lily Horibe; fifth from end, George Kodama and team members.

Yosh: *No.*

Joan: I ask that, because the Cornell Poston Papers said that the government stated that people in camp could send back and get any belongings or furniture they wanted. I wondered whether people really did this.

Yosh: *I do recall that the people my husband's family left their furniture with did bring the washing machine.*

Joan: That was good.

Yosh: *Yes. Because Mother Kodama had six boys. She was scrubbing over the washboard. It was a blessing to get a washing machine. She had four girls; three of them were there and five boys were there.*

Joan: Were any of your children born in camp?

Yosh: *No.*

Joan: Were you pregnant in camp?

Yosh: *No.*

Joan: What kind of recreational activities did you participate in?

Yosh: *Block activities. There were movies and a big screen out in the open like outdoor movies. We all stood, of course. There was no such thing as chairs.*

Joan: For two hours.

Yosh: *We always stood.*

Joan: Did you belong to any groups?

Yosh: *I did join a Red Cross class. I thought it would be a benefit to know something about taking care of anybody who became ill. [She was also on basketball and softball teams.]*

Joan: You worked at a camouflage net factory?

Yosh: *It was inside [the camp]. What we did was run power machines making netting. Our mother applied but you had to be a citizen to work in the camouflage factory.*

Joan: Were you allergic to the dyes?

Yosh: *No, but the power machines ran so fast and were so strong that I was not really very good at it, so I was placed in the cutting room.*

Joan: What do you remember about the Poston strike?*

Yosh: *Not much.*

Joan: When you were a young woman of 19, what about the communication with other Japanese American women?

Yosh: *I think you could say it existed. Then after getting out and everybody going their own way, making a new start, is when there was more communication, I believe, among friends, anyway.*

*Akira Loveridge-Sanbonmatsu, interned at Poston I (1942-1945), explained the strike. "The catalyst for the strike was the decision of the administration to send an alleged assailant of a suspect informant to stand trial in a city outside Poston," October 4, 1999.

Friendships Made

Joan: In other words, the friendships made in camp—you kept those connections. And you wanted to know where people were and to keep up with their lives.

Yosh: Yes.

Joan: There has been a lot of discussion about dust storms.

Yosh: It was terrible. If you were walking from the canteen and a dust storm came up without warning, you'd have to dart into the first barracks available. In fact, when a storm came, everybody just opened their doors for anybody that was walking.

Joan: That was good.

Yosh: You couldn't survive out there, the dust was so bad.

Joan: Wasn't that a little scary?

Yosh: Yes, because we had not ever been subjected to any kind of extreme weather, especially living in the valley [Imperial Valley].

Joan: Did the dust seep into the barracks?

Yosh: Yes. When we first got there the floors had about quarter-inch cracks in them, and of course, the dust came through the windows; up from the floor; and it was awful until they put linoleum in.

Joan: Did people have to mop floors several times a day?

Yosh: We ran hoses on them [the floors]. When we got linoleum, we mopped every day.

Joan: During the dust storms, do you remember the roof ever blowing off the building?

Yosh: One storm blew one end of the building that my husband's family lived in, and all the people went out and got the lumber, and a lot of them made furniture out of redwood, because the wood would have been thrown away.

Joan: But if the roof were blown off, then they had to rebuild?

Yosh: No. The government fixed it.

Joan: I would think the people would be angry at the flimsy structures that were built. What about power outages and water?

Yosh: [The power] was not turned off, but there was no water because of the storm. Power outages were common.

Joan: Have you experienced anything like this since camp?

Yosh: No.

Joan: What hopes did you have for the future?

Yosh: To get out of camp. We realized this was not the real world. We didn't think about the far future.

Joan: What made you decide to go back to Imperial Valley after leaving camp?

Yosh: *Father Kodama decided to go back. [As an elderly Issei*, Takejiro Kodama faced age, economic, and language barriers but had the fortitude to meet the challenge of beginning to farm anew in the valley with his family.] I was staying with my folks in Utah. I did not want to go back to Imperial Valley, but I had no choice in the matter.*

Joan: Testimony in the Cornell Poston Papers stated before January 2, 1945 that the administration actually told people in camps that they shouldn't go back. And that people should not cluster together.

Yosh: *First we went to Colorado to work. Then we went to Utah. But there was such prejudice. They thought we were Chinese so they rented us the motel, with kitchen privileges with another couple. But when they found out we were Japanese, they were looking for any kind of excuse to get us out of there.*

Joan: This was in Utah.

Yosh: *Salt Lake City. George worked as a mechanic and then went into the army for two years. I was pregnant.*

Prejudice and racism reared up again, triggering memories of the prejudice she had suffered in college before camp. Mitamura Kodama now easily identified racism, which resulted in isolation and alienation.

Yosh: *Our son was born in Utah. Then we went back to El Centro [Imperial Valley] and farmed, but the farming practices had changed and it was difficult to adjust and survive. We were forced to quit farming. George went to work for a corporate farm and then retired. Then he came to help in Sanbon, Inc. I worked for the State in the Department of Human Resources [in El Centro and Calexico] and dealt with unemployment and job searches. It's now called Department of Human Development. I worked there for 16 years and retired in 1987.*

Yosh Mitamura Kodama. From camp to Utah.

*Issei is a first generation person born in Japan who moved to the United States and denied the right to United States citizenship.

Yosh's father, Seichi Mitamura on right. Quite a day's catch! Brigham City, Utah. After camp, 1944.

Stories Revealed

Joan: Do you remember any of the stories that were told to you by your mother or your father or grandparents?

Yosh: After camp in fact at our mother's funeral in 1991, the rest of them did not know that it was her second marriage.

Joan: It was important that the stories unfolded, at least for accuracy. When you grew older in camp did you notice if the Japanese culture continued?

Yosh: The Nisei—we were still a young generation, so that the Issei were influential. So that there were more Japanese cultural [activities] offered.

Joan: Did you notice some values which became stronger?

Yosh: Family had always been a strong bond in our family, and I think it continued through camp life and after.

Joan: Were there any cultural values that you felt became less strong?

Yosh: They called us the silent generation because we didn't protest that we were being interned without due process, and our children [Sansei] couldn't understand that. They said, 'Why were you so quiet? Why did you abide by [that]?' They didn't understand the climate of the era during that time.*

Joan: The racism, and the hysteria, hostility.

Yosh: They don't realize that this has changed drastically since the war.

*Sansei are third generation Japanese Americans born in the United States as citizens.

"The wave of race hatred has affected the Japanese in this center" in 1943, according to the "Monthly Report on the Colorado River War Relocation Center for Evacuated Japanese." "Faith has been shaken in the government, in the American People, and in the reality of Democracy. An emotional discharge of hate and fear on the part of the public in the Southwest has recently become evident. The homes of Japanese Americans in California have been broken open and robbed. This stealing… has been the rule in many regions. Moreover, it is apparently being condoned by otherwise responsible civic leaders. People who were formerly anxious to go out and take up their lives again are now intimidated… and depressed." A.H. Leighton concludes, "…the probable ultimate effect of nationwide anti-Japanese feeling stirred up by the administration and political mishandling" will create increased racial antagonism.[2] There were four court cases* that challenged the internment.[3] Furthermore, there were strikes at Poston, Manzanar, and Tule Lake. Congress granted redress for this grievous and unconscionable injustice.[4]

Joan: At what point did you put it (camp) behind you?

Yosh: *I never thought of it being foremost in my mind. It's just that it was life. The war happened. Then the camp happened. I had my child and it's just a series of things that occurred in my life.*

Joan: But how did you let go of your unhappiness?

Yosh: *That went by the wayside after we were in camp for a while. I could see that there were others that felt the same way but they were living with it and accepting it. I guess that's what it was. Just accepting the fact that you can't change it. It was difficult, though. There was no way I could change anything except within myself.*

Joan: Do you remember talking to others about it?

Yosh: *Not so much talking, as my age group was about the same. We were so naïve at nineteen. We lived in a very narrow world. We were so family oriented and had never been away from family, or experienced the so-called outside world.*

Legacies

Joan: What are your thoughts about how this could be prevented in future generations in the U.S.?

Yosh: *Oh, the way people are now, I don't think anybody would be subjected to internment as a mass, like it was in '42.*

Joan: I certainly hope not. Do you think there are ways to make sure that this won't happen again?

Yosh: *Personally, you know the JACL [Japanese American Citizens League] is working on it not recurring. If there were any signs of it, they'd immediately address it. We benefit from their actions.*

*The four cases are Mitsuye Endo, Gordon Hirabayashi, Fred Korematsu, and Minoru Yasui. These cases are discussed in *Japanese American History.*

Joan: I know that there are still incidents of violence, hostility and racism, and I think *The Pacific Citizen* (newspaper of JACL) does a really good job of reporting those. On a different note, what happened last month at the Imperial County Historical Museum?

Yosh: *The Japanese American ethnic galleries museum [the exhibition is called Japanese American Gallery] opening was a success wholly due to the cooperation of everybody who used to live here, and the ones that are living here now. Primarily the resources have come from people who lived here in the valley, and they're honoring their parents.*

Joan: I heard that it was a tremendous success. That you really did so much work. Can you describe the museum a little bit?

Yosh: *It's professionally co-ordinated by Tim Asamen* who is president of the Japanese American ethnic group [the exhibit is called Japanese American Gallery in the Pioneers' Museum]. They spent $28,000 for the initial exhibition. They really put themselves out. I think we have a lot of untapped resources.*

Joan: What is the nature of the exhibits?

Yosh: *Basically, it's to honor our parents, and their work and their values that they instilled in all of us. It's not surprising that people—like today, we went to look at the Guest Book, and there were at least ten Japanese names in there who came for that purpose. They do make an effort and they stop to see the names.*

Joan: And the museum is located?

Yosh: *It's on the road right across from the Imperial Valley College. It's between El Centro and Imperial, about two miles east of the main road that goes to Los Angeles north.*

Joan: What were the turning points in your life recently?

Yosh: *The death of George [her husband] on July 26, 1991; my job for the state, and joining the El Centro Regional Medical Center Auxiliary when George died.*

Yoshiko Mitamura Kodama talked about the distress she felt at being forced into camp at age nineteen. She had to find a way to let this feeling go. Seeing other people feel and endure the same desolation gave her the courage to shake the unhappiness and apprehension from her shoulders like water from a summer rain. Yosh Mitamura, raised in Imperial Valley, was not accustomed to the extremes in the weather. The dust storms were "terrifying because we had not ever been subjected to any kind of extreme weather."

*Tim Asamen serves as Chair and Coordinator of the Japanese American Gallery in the Imperial Valley Pioneers' Museum from 1991 to the present. He served on the Imperial County Historical Society (ICHS) Board of Directors 1997—2004. In addition, Asamen served as President of the ICHS in 2001 as well as on the Executive Board (1999—2004).

The discrimination she remembers. Upon leaving camp, she and her husband, George, traveled to Utah. "There was such prejudice," she reiterates. The motel owners rented to them because they thought they were Chinese. When they discovered that Yosh and George were Japanese, they found any excuse to force them to leave.

At camp, she made lifelong friends. "After getting out and everybody going their own way, making a new start, is when there was more communication, I believe, among friends, anyway," she commented. She valued the friendships she made in camp, and wanted to keep those connections. When people are in adverse situations, the friendships made cement together and often become lasting. Such was the case with Yoshiko Mitamura Kodama. Pride exudes from her voice when she speaks of the opening of the Imperial Valley Japanese American Gallery at the Imperial County Historical Society Pioneers' Museum, a time at which her parents were honored in the exhibits. She has continuously supported the Japanese American community and now serves as Treasurer of the Japanese American Citizens League, Imperial Valley Chapter. Indeed, she considers herself "blessed."

George Kodama

*Yoshiko Mitamura Kodama, El Centro, California.
April 30, 2005.*

When cottonwood trees
grow, then the yellow-breasted
meadow larks will sing

木々育ち
黄金の草原
ヒバリ鳴く

Ki-gi so-da-chi
ko-ga-ne no so-u-ge-n
hi-ba-ri na-ku

RURI TSUCHIYA ISHIMARU'S TESTIMONY*

"When the trees grow, the birds come."
"I didn't know where to go. We stayed [at Poston] until the very last."

When Ruri Tsuchiya, as a Kibei†, returned to the United States in 1932, she could have been regarded as aloof, and a foreigner, with adjustment problems. Instead, she fit in and quickly assumed the role of eldest in the family, sister and helping to raise the children. Ruri Tsuchiya, like many other Kibei, returned to the U.S. in her late teens (nineteen years old). Sometimes only the eldest child was sent back to Japan, a common practice. The Kibei became a minority within a minority. Kibei were not only different from Americans in speech and customs but they were different from Nisei Japanese Americans, in speech, education, and customs.[1]

Ruri Tsuchiya came back to five brothers, five strangers. She had to learn English and the American ways. She had not seen her mother Teru Tsuchiya Sanbonmatsu in sixteen years. Moreover, the five brothers had never been to Japan. She took English classes at the high school, and taught Japanese classes at the church.

Joan: Here in the United States, your mother raised the children.

Ruri: In the Christian way. Maybe because we are so brought up with the Japanese Buddhism, so even if the Japanese say Christian ideas, in their heart and soul there are Buddhist ideas.

Joan: When your father died, your mother took over the business? What business was that?

Ruri: A produce business. Also the farming. The crops were tomatoes, squash, lettuce. Buying vegetables and sending them to Los Angeles and Chicago or New York. It's more like gambling.

Joan: Gambling in the sense that if the weather is bad that really affects the produce.

*The reader needs to be aware that several original documents exist for this work: three oral histories taken over a period of years, 1983--1994; transcriptions of audio recordings completed by Betty Restuccia of Oral Histories I and III; the final document which included clarifications and some brief additions by her son, Mikio, and daughter-in-law, Vickie Ishimaru, since Ruri died in 1997 before the completion of this book.

†Kibei are second generation Japanese Americans born in the United States as citizens but educated in Japan.

Ruri:	*Yes. She [her mother] let people pack in our shed. We did packing, too. Quite a number of people working, sometimes 300, and Mother just overseeing how they were doing. We had a foreman taking care of those things, but also Mother knew much more than the foreman because she could read the newspapers and she had a ledger and could find the dollars and cents. Those Japanese foremen, they can't get the knowledge from the ledger. But my mother could…**
Joan:	Did she have both men and women working?
Ruri:	*Mostly men. My father was very nice to people so they felt sorry for my mother so they try to help her. Of course, there was a lot of resentment because my mother was a female.*
Joan:	I was wondering about that.
Ruri:	*So I think she really had a hard time. Those men, they don't like to take orders from my mother. She didn't have any relatives in this country when my father was alive. She never went out into the fields or to buy groceries or even buy her personal things. Father went to the store to buy for her. Because every year she had a baby. Father was very nice to her because it was really nice to have a good wife in America. I mean in those days, very hard to get a good wife. A good wife means a Japanese wife, a Japanese woman.*

Teru Tsuchiya and toddler Ruri Tsuchiya. Japan, about 1916.

Earlier Years in Japan and Then America

In Ruri's earlier years, she was left with her grandmother to be educated in Japan. After her father's death, her mother married Yoshimitsu Sanbonmatsu and returned to the United States The sequence follows.

Ruri:	*I am the eldest. My mother took me to Japan. I was only three years old.*
Joan:	How long were you there?
Ruri:	*I went to grammar school, girls college—Tokyo Girls College—and then came here.*[2]
Joan:	How did your parents meet?
Ruri:	*You see, my mother came to this country to study; my father came to study in medical school (at Stanford), so both met in San Francisco, and they married.*

*Ruri Tsuychia was educated in Japan. The grammatical structure and Japanese tone of her English have been preserved.

Joan: Your mother was very independent. She must have been a strong woman.

Ruri: Yes, she was.

Joan: To come to this country where she didn't know the language, to try to continue her schooling. Was she able to get into college?

Ruri: Oh, no. My grandfather was very angry so he cut the complete family ties with her, so my mother had to borrow the money to come to the United States. She had to work to repay the money she borrowed. Those days, schoolgirls got two or three dollars a month. She never worked in Japan. She was from a wealthy family.*

Joan: So that was a big difference, because in Japan she was a member of a class that had people working in her house, and here in the United States, she worked. What kind of similarities were there between the way you were a mother and the way your mother was a mother?

Ruri: It was very different. She had nobody; just her husband—my father—and he wasn't wealthy because his family cut his money allowance on account of his marriage to my mother. He had to work, too, and those days wages are very low. He started to tailor because he could read English and import lots of things from Japan. He didn't have any suits so my father started to sew and that was the easiest way to make money.

Joan: As far as being a parent, how did you see yourself?

Ruri: I think almost the same, but before there was a big difference with my grandmother and mother. My mother could show her love to a child, directly; most of the times they had a nursemaid, and the mother couldn't take care of her own child, as they say now in the upper class.

Joan: So there was a distance between your mother and her mother.

Ruri: My mother carried me, and I do love and take care of my son almost the same.

Joan: What was a typical day when you were five or six years old? You would have been in Japan at that time.

Ruri: Every day, play paper dolls, bean bags, and some cards. Most of the time stick around my grandmother or grandfather.

Joan: Did you all live in the same house?

Ruri: Oh yes, but my aunt [Fuku Tsuchiya] and great grandfather and great grandmother lived in a different location in a different town, a little town, because they were completely retired; a very small very convenient house. They had just one maid. My grandfather's house was very large; my grandmother, grandfather, and two uncles, two aunties, three maids and two servants. It was a big house. On my mother's side, my grandmother's name was Ryu Ohara Tsuchiya.

*Note by son, Mikio and Vickie Ishimaru: Ruri told us that her grandfather had paid for her mother (Teru) to come to the United States and continue her education. We believe her mother [Teru] got married shortly after arriving in the United States and was cut off as a result.

Ruri and brother, Koichi, growing up in Japan.

Joan: What expectations did your mother have for you?

Ruri: At my aunt's high school, there was a beautiful teacher, Fumiko Imi. She had a beautiful voice and she always read poems and Japanese stories. I would just adore her. My aunt who taught at that high school was named Fuku Tsuchiya.

Joan: I wonder if there were any books about women which you read in your younger days.

Ruri: I read lots of books about girls, stories by Yoshiya Noko who was very popular in those days. I read Madame Curie, Helen Keller.

Joan: At what age did you start thinking about your future?

Ruri: I think when I was very small, very, very young, about five or six years old, I wanted to be a department store keeper and a painter. When I would go to the department store and say how nice if I were the owner of this store, [then] I could have everything I wanted. My mother wanted me to be a nice woman, a nice wife, because that's where real happiness for a woman is. I didn't believe this. My grandfather wanted me to be a teacher or some professional. At school, I was always tops in the painting class. I said to my heart,

it's nice to be a painter; all my life
with my eyes, I don't have to do anything;
just paint, paint, paint.

Joan: After you finished high school, which was in Japan—

Ruri: *Yes, and I went to my girls' college. There my eyes opened up; had very good teachers. I saw many of my grammar school classmates were brides, but didn't have the money to go to high school. Our class [in high school] was only 30 and only 2 girls. I studied very hard in high school and college. I couldn't enjoy good times with light-hearted people because I was always thinking about friends who were poor.*

Joan: You almost felt like you had a sense of responsibility to learn, to pass that knowledge on. When you finished college, you came back to the U.S. What year was that?

Ruri: *1932.*

Joan: Between 1932 and 1941 what happened?

Ruri: *Those days I helped my mother. Took care of my brothers. [She taught Japanese for nine years at the church in El Centro, 1933-1942]. My uncle in Japan thought the children should go back to Japan, but my mother said, "no" because it is so much easier to get a college education for the boys.*

Joan: In your family, before you married, if there were family disagreements how were these worked out?

Ruri: *Every time I wanted to go back to Japan, Momma got sick and that's how. Psychologists say you can't stay with your brothers too many years. And your mother will die, and your brothers will get married. What are you going to do when you get old? But anyway, finally, I decided to get married to Tsukumo. Mother was happy at first, but I had to leave home. Oh, she really got mad at me, but I couldn't do anything but just leave. That was*

Ruri, don't always think about Momma. Just maybe humor her; she will overcome it.

Joan: You had your own life to lead, and then, probably after Mikio (her son) came, maybe your mother…

Ruri: *Yes.*

Joan: With the baby coming, things might get better?

Ruri: *Yes. But Tsukumo didn't like the idea. I felt sorry for Momma, but that's the way. She was very particular about my brothers' girlfriends. Momma was a very strong person. You know one of my friends said, 'You know, Ruri, I don't like to tell you, but after your mother's funeral, all these boys can marry.'*

Joan: That's very interesting because your mother was really a strong person, and she left Japan against her family's wishes in Japan and then you in turn are a strong woman because you made a decision to marry Tuskumo even though it was difficult and she did not like it. You were a strong person and you left.

Ruri: *Maybe so.*

Kibei women tended to marry Kibei and Issei men rather than Nisei.[3] Ruri married Tsukumo Ishimaru, Kibei, in spring of 1942.

Pearl Harbor and Evacuation

Joan: When Pearl Harbor happened, where were you?

Ruri: I was home in Holtville, cooking dinner when I heard it on the radio. I felt sad. I had mixed feelings.

Joan: When the notification posters to evacuate were being nailed up, where were you?

Ruri: It was printed in the Japanese newspapers. I read it there. I didn't see the posters nailed up.

Joan: When you left Holtville, did you have to destroy things which were Japanese like dishes, scrolls, books?

Ruri: We gave away our belongings. Some were kept in a Buddhist Temple, but they were stolen. The coast people near Los Angeles started moving within twenty-four hours after Pearl Harbor. So hard. Everything. They just left.

Joan: What happened to your mother's home?

Ruri: Two months notice—evacuate. So all farming had to stop. Just left and all farm equipment and the house also…

Joan: Did you get paid for the land?

*Ruri: I don't think so. I went back. Nothing left. Everything was gone from the house. [none of her belongings were in the house.]**

Joan: When everyone had to move out, did everyone go together?

Ruri: Yes. All went to the bus and we could take 5 to 10 pounds of belongings.

Joan: And you didn't know if you were coming back.

Ruri: That's right.

Ruri Tsuchiya-back row. Front L-R Yoshiya, Yoshiro, dog Rex, mother Teru, seated; Akira in front, behind Akira, Kozo; Mitsuo, far right. Holtville, CA about 1935.

*According to Akira Loveridge-Sanbonmatsu who returned from camp to the Sanbonmatsu homestead, the house had not been sold. The farm equipment had been stored and was still intact.

Arrival at Poston

Joan: What do you remember about that day of going to camp?

Ruri: It was a real hot day, maybe 110°. No air conditioning. There was nothing but sand. No trees, no grass, just bare. Tarred roof, a big army barracks. There were no birds, but lots of ants on the ground. It was so hot I remember my foot, just to dip it into the sand, sinking one toe by one toe and it was so hot. And I remember the evening, when we got our number—21152D. Each one had a number like a prisoner. It was like a luggage tag pinned on my coat. And we got our barracks. We all lived in one room, my family. We lived, my mother-in-law, father-in-law, my two brothers-in-law, and my sister-in-law and my husband and I. We were lucky. Only seven in a room. Other families had three families in one room. There were no springs [in the] beds. We had to put straw into the canvas bag and had one army blanket. And the straw was so dusty and I wasn't used to all that dust. The evening was so hot.

Joan: Probably the bathroom was down the street.

Ruri: Yes. They were tin barracks. There was one for men and one for women and no partition between toilet walls.

Joan: No privacy.

Ruri: No privacy. And just showers, no bathtub. There was no laundry room, and only one kitchen. Camp. It was a horrible experience.*

Joan: Were there any support groups or classes or orientation?

Ruri: Later on. At the beginning, all camp instructors thought that the Japanese were uneducated. But they found out most were college graduates or college students. Just a very few only high school. Most went to college. Japanese standards very high.

Camp Life

Joan: I wonder about the women in camp. When they worked, did they get paid?

Ruri: Sixteen dollars a month. A chef in the kitchen got $19.00. Department heads, the newspaper editors, the same.

Joan: Were women able to get the positions which paid $19.00?

Ruri: I don't think there were any.

Joan: So it was men who were paid $19.00.

Ruri: Yes.

*The Japanese bath is more than washing oneself; it is a cultural and spiritual custom.

Joan: That's interesting. What kind of food did you eat?

Ruri: Oh, food. The food was very poor. Mostly dried fruits and meat, and very short on meat, and the milk was dry milk and canned beans. I was pregnant when I came to camp. There was no proper diet—no fresh fruit. The first 6 months were tough. Later we raised chickens and vegetables. We produced good fresh vegetables there. We had enough chickens for one a week, almost a…*

Joan: A community.

Ruri: Yes.

Joan: Were you able to eat like a family, in your room?

Ruri: Oh, no. Yes, supposed to, but no. Young people go first in the mess hall and they are all in their own groups, sit down and eat, and finish first and then go out and play. And every month all children get $3.50 a month allowance for clothing. That's big money because you have enough food. They don't have to ask their parents for allowance. They don't listen. The children don't listen what to do, what to not do. They love to play, always.

Joan: They didn't have supervision or even models of eating with their elders or their parents because the children ate together.

Ruri: And most times, they don't go home early enough. They just stay out in the fields playing basketball or baseball or some played cards.

Joan: In other words, some people have mixed feelings. Teenagers like to be with their friends. There was probably a solidarity of feeling together.

Ruri: Yes.

Joan: How was Japanese culture continued in camp?

Ruri: There were classical dance, Kabuki, koto, *and other musical instruments were played. At the camp, my father-in-law made a stringed instrument, the* biwa, *from a tree, and Tsukumo's mother played it.*

It was probably easy for Ruri Tsuchiya Ishimaru to communicate with her husband's parents because of her ability to speak Japanese. In fact, Kibei were often a liaison between Issei and Nisei.

Joan: I have read some accounts of the dust storms and wonder how the dust storms affected you.

*Leighton reported that the food allowance would be reduced from 41 cents per day to 31 cents, a bare subsistence level.[4]

Ruri: *They were awful. One day, about three o'clock, suddenly, the sky clouded, and thunderstorms came. You can't breathe or anything. It was so hot; put the wet towel on your face. It just swept down in thirty minutes. The sky got real dark, when the dust storm came. The dust comes and you can't breathe. It happened quite often when we first came, but later we put big trees and lawns in and everything and we started farming and building.*

Joan: To hold down the dust. That's interesting. Did the dust storms bother Mikio's asthma?

Ruri: *He wasn't born yet. I worked in the mess hall before he was born.*

Joan: Was Mikio born in camp?

Ruri: *Yes. 1943.*

Joan: Did you belong to the women's clubs?

Ruri: *No. I didn't because I was taking care of the baby. I did take a sewing class, and I taught flower arrangement.*

Joan: I wonder if Mikio got any of the children's illnesses.

Ruri: *We had a hospital and a Japanese doctor. You had to wait in line for the doctor, for everything.*

Joan: I wonder how you thought Japanese American women communicated with each other.

Ruri: *We eat together at the mess hall, and saw each other at the shower and toilets, so we had to meet whether we like it or not. We waited in line for everything. There was communication talking about children or our husbands.*

Joan: Were the men involved in childcare?

Ruri: *Oh, yes.*

Joan: Was there a fence around the camp?

Ruri: *Yes, just in front. Back was nothing, but we had the creek and the desert, just desert. It was very hot.*

Joan: I understand at times it was 128°.

Ruri: *It was so hot you could fry eggs on the roof.*

Joan: Do you remember the strike?

Ruri: *Yes. It was November; November 17, 1942—for several days.*

Joan: I read that the government said there would be air conditioning and beds; that people could bring their own furniture.

Ruri: *Oh, no. We couldn't have any furniture. No air conditioning.*

Ruri Tsuchiya Isimaru and baby Mikio in Poston camp, 1943.

Leaving Camp and Moving On

Ruri: *When we went, [to camp], there was nothing, but the first year, we got lawns and trees. The Japanese people worked very hard and even put in the water. [We] made a very good grammar school and high school.*

Joan: The community was transformed.

Ruri: *Very nice, really, really. [You] couldn't imagine. When we had to leave, lots of people didn't want to move because everything so centered. We had a beautiful auditorium. We had a Japanese garden. When the trees grow, the birds come. Oh, there was quite a number of wild horses, and Mikio [their baby son] said, 'Aah, Mommy, look at that. There's a doggie. There's a doggie' [laughter]. I told him that's a horse. I said [to myself],*

Oh, oh. He can't experience those. We have to get out. We can't stay here.

Joan: As you were preparing to leave camp, did any events happen?

Ruri *My father-in-law died. A Buddhist priest conducted the funeral and photos were taken with special cameras.*

Then came the leaving of camp and resettlement.

Ruri Tsuchiya Isimaru playing with Mikio in Poston camp, Arizona, about 1944.

Resettlement

As victims of racism, there was fear of the undertow of discrimination in both Issei and Nisei. The anti-Japanese groups such as the American Legion, Native Sons of the Golden West, and the *Denver Post* were increasing in number. The Nisei were anxious to find a suitable job which paid reasonable wages. For the Nisei, the selection of the job to reflect interest, schooling, and experience was a challenge. In the beginning, most of the jobs were domestic and menial, such as gardener, housecleaner, or farmhand. The Nisei reflected more optimism.

Although Ruri Tsuchiya Ishimaru had many challenges in resettling, her philosophy and optimism underscored her life as she grappled with the problems.

Joan: When you came out of camp, were there problems finding a job?

Ruri: Very, very much. I stayed until the very last. We didn't know where to go, so Tsukumo [Ruri's spouse] wrote letters to New Haven, Connecticut, and the mayor sent us a welcome note. So I said, 'Well, let's go to New Haven.' They gave us two tickets to New Haven and one week's allowance. Tsukumo went to Chicago on the way to New Haven and met a friend and he stayed in Chicago a couple of days with friends. On the way to New Haven, he stopped in New York. He couldn't find an apartment.

Joan: Why was it so hard?

Ruri: Children. Finally he found an apartment, a small one-room apartment that was better than nothing, so he called me.

Ruri: We [Ruri and Mikio] went to New York and stayed about 9 years, but my son had asthma. We thought maybe Hawaii is a better place to go but we stopped in Chicago to see my friend.

Resettling the West Coast evacuees proved to be more difficult than the War Relocation Authority (WRA) thought. When the time came that Japanese Americans could leave, California, Washington and Oregon were not options at that time. The WRA wondered why they weren't leaving by droves. Toshio Yatsushiro and Iwao Ishino conducted a poll. Suprising results were discovered. While most Nisei were planning to resettle, most of the Issei were not. The Issei wanted to stay longer, or were undecided. Four factors emerged: economic difficulties, difficulty in securing a job, fear of discrimination, and family problems.

For the Issei, age was one problem. One elderly Issei said, " 'I am too old; my body does not mind me anymore.' "[5] The Issei wanted to return to the West Coast. Having to start all over was terrifying to them. They had been uprooted from their foundations in the evacuation, but that foundation still represented a little piece of security. The feelings of fear, anxiety, and anger intensified.

According to Yatsushiro and Ishino, "The problem of resettlement does not end with the evacuee leaving, but really begins there, for he [or she] will be confronted with innumerable readjustment problems. Whereas evacuation was a hasty military operation, resettlement demands deep insight as well as foresight. Resettlement is a challenging invitation to freedom for the evacuees and an equally challenging responsibility of the government and the American people. It is a crucial test of the basic principles of American democracy as set forth by the Constitution and the Four Freedoms."[6]

The evacuees were released with the policy that they must not congregate into *Little Tokyos.* Moreover, they should not walk down the street four abreast. Although clusters already appeared in Salt Lake City, Denver, and Chicago, Yatsushiro asserted that evacuees are no different from other groups in a community who need a sense of belonging.[7]

Nisei may leave but they will not take with them their younger brothers and sisters. Living in the camp for these tender children is not just a passing affair... Living in a relocation center environment long enough during their formative years, these children will feel the evacuation and all its consequences in their lifetime.[8]

Although physical wounds may heal in a short time, the deep psychological wounds from evacuation and incarceration tend to linger over a lifetime, and require a continuous and frequent treatment like a chronic illness. The self-confidence and self-respect which was swept away by the evacuation needs to be regained. Like divers who go through a decompression chamber, there needs to be an adjustment process which recognizes the stages by which people will recover from this survival in the depths.[9]

Ruri, son Mikio, and husband, Tsuku...
New York City, late 1940's–early 195...

New York City and Chicago

Joan: Before you moved here (at Heiwa Terrace in Chicago) you lived in other locations. What were some of those places?

*Ruri: After the war, we went to New York and stayed there about nine [seven] years, [where they worked in and later bought a dry cleaning business] and then we liked New York, very much, too, but my son had asthma [and urban renewal was taking over many businesses].**

Joan: You lived there nine [seven] years?

Ruri: Yes.

Joan: And then what happened?

*Mikio and Vickie Ishimaru clarified that they believe it was about "seven years, based on photos we have of Mikio in 3rd grade in a Chicago elementary school." They moved due to urban renewal in New York.

Ruri: *We stopped in Chicago to see my friend, and we had a very good doctor for Mikio. They have a Children's Memorial Hospital. They have wonderful doctors so we decided to stay here.*

In Chicago, Ruri and Tsukumo worked in and later owned a dry cleaning business. Later, Ruri Tsuchiya Ishimaru worked as a clerk in a business while raising their son. In 1967, she visited Japan to reconnect with all her relatives. Upon retirement, the Ishimarus moved to Heiwa Terrace in Chicago, a retirement community. Japanese Americans contributed funds, as did the government and Japanese companies. It's a community of Asian and Asian American families who help each other in their retirement years.

Joan Loveridge-Sanbonmatsu

Ruri and Tsukumo, retired. Japanese Garden at Heiwa Terrace, Chicago. Early 1990s.

Joan: Heiwa Terrace, what does that mean?

Ruri: *Peaceful. We have nutrition class, art classes, photograph-taking class, pottery, bonsai, tea ceremony, haiku, and special exercises for health. I have a fine number of friends in this building. We have a shopping district in walking distance. Very convenient. All kinds of people here, retired professors and medical doctors.*

Joan: There's a diverse educational level.

Ruri: *Older people have a lot of knowledge with their living experiences.*

Joan: Did you as parents in raising Mikio want Mikio to learn Japanese or some Japanese culture?

Ruri: *To tell the truth, I never think about any of those things. I just wanted him to be healthy.*[10]

Joan: Well, he went to the University of Illinois and majored in engineering, and then went on to law school.

Ruri: *We had very good friends, all Japanese friends—were well educated, cultured, very respectable persons, so that makes a lot of difference for Mikio. Now, he's a lawyer and he's doing very well. He's a patent lawyer.*[11]

Joan: Here in Chicago there is a large Japanese and Japanese American community, and some of the cultural traditions you keep in your home. That must have had an influence on Mikio.

Ruri: *Yes. I think so.*

Joan: Everyone in the community put forth a lot of energy. Do you still measure your life by the yardstick of the camp experience?

Ruri: *No. I don't know. [Pause] I don't think… The bitterness, I think I experienced, too.*

Joan: You've put it behind you. At what point do you remember putting it behind you?

Ruri: *I don't recall.*

Joan: So you never lost your memory of it.

Ruri: *I did respect all the Japanese people. We tried our best to help each other. It was so hard right after the war when we came out. It was so hard to rent a house. Also, young people didn't have a decent job, even a college graduate just cleaning job, domestic job. The people have discrimination for the Japanese.*

Joan: People were demoralized. Because they had an education, they were trained to do a professional job, and the only job, because of racial discrimination, was to be a domestic or a gardener.

Ruri: *Yes.*

Joan: Do you remember being told in camp not to return to California?

Ruri: *I don't remember. I was just busy with Mikio and with other families with children.*

Joan: In resettlement times, I read, there was a ban on returning to California, not to congregate in groups, or walk 4 or 5 abreast down the street. Only a few courageous families returned to the Imperial Valley area.

Ruri: *I think so. That's why people came to Chicago.*

Joan: I wonder how you see yourself now.

Ruri: *We could bear it [camp]. Three and a half years was such a long time. Things were not the best of conditions.*

Joan: So you saw yourselves and other Japanese Americans start their lives all over again and live through all of this and survive.

Ruri: *That's right.*

Joan: That's important. Meeting new Japanese Americans (in camp) perhaps gave you some idea of where you might like to live. In other words, that you might like to live in a city that had Japanese Americans.

Ruri: *Ah, yes. You see we picked the area [in Chicago] based on common language, so anybody, even a stranger, will speak in Japanese. This gives us some kind of warmness. It was hard.*

Joan: But you didn't give up.

Ruri: *I was really surprised! In camp, lots of sick people were very old, and they had lost everything they had built, but still they had the courage to think about the future and their children. There really was courage!*

Up to this point we can see discrimination on two accounts, race and gender. A European American librarian in camp, for example, received $167.00 a month while her Japanese American counterpart was paid $16.00 a month.[12] Among Japanese Americans at camp, the women were not eligible for the chef position or newspaper editor position which paid $19.00 a month in contrast to $16.00 a month.[13]

There has been so much emphasis on life in camp that one might wonder if there were life before camp. Ruri Tsuchiya Ishimaru had taught Japanese language classes in El Centro at the El Centro Christian Church, worked for the *Rafu Shimpo* newspaper as a part-time reporter for the county of Imperial, earning $30.00 a month. College educated in Japan, with an interest in art, she had been mentored by her favorite high school teacher, Fumiko Imi, who read poetry and classic Japanese stories, and her auntie, Fuku Tsuchiya. She was one of two girls in her high school class. Her grandmother, Ryu Ohara Tsuchiya, urged her to go to college so that she could be more independent than she was. Upon graduation from Tokyo Women's College, she willingly came back to the United States to help her mother raise five boys. She nurtured her five brothers in such ways as taking Kozò Sanbonmatsu to special art classes. Although raised Christian, in her heart, "there were Buddhist ideas." She was also an active member of the Japanese American Citizens League. In the fall, she married Tsukumo Ishimaru and they lived in their own apartment in El Centro. Upon entering Camp Poston, she faced horrendous living conditions. From the worst possible conditions of living they transformed this barren desert into a more bearable quality of life.

Ruri's son, Mikio and family.
Front row, L-R, Mikio and Vickie
Second row, L-R: David Ishimaru, Ann Miho Ishimaru, Karen Ishimaru
Back row, L-R: Zack Semke, Ann's spouse; Nghi (Tin) Nguyen, Karen's spouse
Sunnyvale, California, about 2000.

Keeping hope rekindled in camp and resettlement was difficult in such trying times, but she demonstrated over and over, that she held hope in her hand. Perhaps she saw some of the elderly Japanese as role models. She spoke with admiration and pride about resiliency, patience, and hard work of the Japanese Americans. "In camp, lots of sick people were very old and they had lost everything they had built, but still they had the courage to think about the future and their children. There was really courage."

Chapter 6

THE TRANSCENDENT SPIRIT

"If I can get through camp, I can get through anything," noted Mabel Kawashima Ota. Camp has not been forgotten by each of the interviewees. Yatsushiro and Ishimo wrote, "As one evacuee put it: 'The relocation center is a psychological nightmare and a physical hell hole.'"[1]

Gambaru

To transcend Poston, one of the more important aspects may be the value or personal quality of "*gambaru.*" It is what got people through [camp]. "It is a Japanese word," explains Kiku Hori Funabi from Heart Mountain Camp [Wyoming] "for which there is no equivalent. It means to fight, to have courage, to persevere. *Gambaru* is our heritage which is rooted in America. *Gambaru* is a legacy which courageous women and men left us, all of us. This quality is their contribution to America."[2]

The Struggle

These five women projected willingness to tell their stories about camp: their alienation, wretched food, and depression. They told of their uprooting and incarceration, of day-to-day frustrations, lack of privacy and amenities. "It was a shocking experience to arrive there and step into all that dust," Mabel Kawashima Ota reflected. Then like aftershocks of an earthquake, she was to learn that her baby had brain damage due to the lack of medical care. Another aftershock came with the misdiagnosis of her father, leading to his death. These life-changing events motivated her to make decisions which would become crossroads in her life. These women confronted hurdle after hurdle, and overcame.

Three women were already married and were pregnant in camp. As Ruri Tsuchiya Ishimaru emphasized, "It was very tough, no proper diet, no fresh fruit," as did Shigematsu Hoshizaki. Thus, issues of birthing, medical care and health and childcare confronted them head on.

These five women ranged in ages fifteen to twenty-eight. Three of the five women lived in Block 39, known for its individualism. One lived in Block 6 and Block 5, and one lived in Block 60. One woman, Mitamura Kodama, fell in love and got married in camp.

Communication, Networks and Roles

Communication patterns, or lack of patterns of communication, emerged both within camp and after camp. Within camp, proximity gave women easy access to each other. The laundry, the kitchen, the bathroom, the dining room (mess hall)—these spaces lent themselves to communication. Tsuchiya Ishimaru observed, "We eat together at the mess hall, and saw each other at the showers and toilets, so we had to meet whether we like it or not. We waited in line for everything. She said, "There was communication about children or husband."

Yoshiko Mitamura Kodama thought communication existed in camp, but intensified upon leaving camp. These relationships enriched her life.

An example of noncommunication surfaced on the milk issue. Obviously, the administration didn't listen very well to Shigematsu Hoshizaki when she arrived at camp with a hungry baby and could not get milk.

If women's networks developed during the women's clubs and mothers' clubs meetings, and there were no day care centers so they could attend these meetings, young mothers might be left out of the loop. However, informal networks evolved. Tsuchiya Ishimaru commented that she didn't belong to the clubs because "I was taking care of the baby." Mary Shigematsu Hoshizaki indicated that with two small children and a third infant born in camp, she didn't go out. "There was no support group," she said. She felt isolated. Her husband worked in Utah while she stayed in camp to care for the three small children. Without support groups, coping and managing would be very difficult, indeed. Mitamura Kodama pointed out that she communicated more outside of camp, after she left. "Then, after getting out and everybody going their own way, making a new start, is when there was more communication."

In looking at communication patterns, those who were Kibei like Ruri Tsuchiya Ishimaru, would be more likely to have communication with their parents and other Issei because of their facility to speak Japanese fluently. The other women who were Nisei may have been learning Japanese, such as Yoshiko and Mary Mitamura (Nisei) so that they could communicate better with their Issei parents. Shigematsu Hoshizaki also took Japanese classes in El Centro before camp. When she spoke to her parents, she spoke in Japanese. Kawashima Ota disclosed that she got to know Japanese of all ages. She developed more empathy for the Issei and their problems. Besides the communication patterns were the roles.

Women's roles seemed to expand. Women pitched right in on the project of building a school, actually making the adobe bricks. In addition to the traditional values of childcare and eldercare giving and housekeeping responsibilities, women's roles grew. They stepped out of their traditional roles. They formed women's clubs and mother's clubs and ran for the community council and won.

In contrast, men were reluctant to expand their roles to include childcare and housekeeping, although some helped with childcare. They were disinclined also when enlisted to help with the heavy laundry.

Reliance on Family and Cultural Values

Some values faded, such as eating meals together around a table, due to the structure of the camp. Kawashima Ota commented that cultural values weakened. Mitamura Sanbonmatsu specified, "Until we went to camp, my parents were always after us about education." The camp environment did not motivate students to study. She continued, "We were living sort of suspended. You went day by day. We had no ambition." This was one of the costs of camp. However, in Mitamura's family, they ate meals together. "My folks insisted on that. We are very strong about family." This must have been due to the fact that both parents were alive and well. Ruri Tsuchiya Ishimaru observed that many young people ate together and not with their families.

Young people loved being with young people. This, combined with a government allowance, set a pattern for children not having to work for an allowance but still having money, which added fuel to the attitude of not listening to their parents. This appeared to have underminded some family values. Nevertheless, for many Japanese Americans, it was the first time in their lives in which they interacted with so many Japanese Americans. This probably would have strengthened the values of unity, togetherness, and communication. However, now Sansei, or third generation Japanese Americans, are bewildered that many Issei and Nisei would cling to the traditional value of silence, silence about camp. Mitamura Kodama commented, "We didn't protest that we were being interned without due process, and our children couldn't understand that. They said, 'Why were you so quiet?'" However, on November 14, 1942, a massive strike took place.[3]

Another value, friendship, was accentuated by Mitamura Kodama. Friendships made in camp were lifelong. Friendships endure, even to this day. Tsuchiya Ishimaru recalled that the Japanese culture was carried on in camp by many of the women, especially after people settled in. Japanese classes were held. She, herself, taught Japanese flower arranging in camp, and before camp, Japanese language classes. Classical dance, *Kabuki* (drama), talent shows, Judo, Japanese New Year celebrations, *Zori*-making (straw sandal), tea ceremony, and wood carving classes were given. Her mother-in-law played the *biwa*, a musical instrument. Buddhist and Christian churches were formed. In short, one role in which women saw themselves was that of carriers of the culture.

Equally important is the value of positiveness emphasized by Mary Mitamura when dealt with a negative situation. Not only did Mitamura Sanbonmatsu develop a sense of humor but she also developed an optimistic philosophy toward life which sustains her today. She declares, "And I don't think it has anything to do with age" (She was the youngest—a teenager in high school in camp—of the five women interviewed). "Plant the seed of positiveness and empower people. I want people to be strong and independent." Mitamura Sanbonmatsu today sees herself as a troubleshooter, and very practical.

Educational Challenges

Most importantly, education, a cultural value, was demonstrated by the building of their own schools. Poston I, II and III did this. On the other hand, the other camps in the United States did not. Even though there was no heat at 32°F nor air conditioning at 130°F, or books, tables, chairs, there was a curriculum. Granted the classes took place at one end of campus, then the other end, and students would have to drag their chairs all the way across the campus. And, if the college preparation classes were really far away, students' motivation floundered since they could never make it to class on time. Moreover, their advisement was geared not toward college but toward vocational classes.

Learning to let go of the negativity was the challenge for Mitamura Kodama and Shigematsu Hoshizaki. They had been openly discriminated against as had Kawashima Ota. Tshuchiya Ishimaru felt discrimination also. Shigematsu Hoshizaki remembered when she and her spouse, George, came out of camp with three children, no one wanted to rent to them. They didn't have anything nor anywhere to live, so they lived in a vacant building. Kawashima Ota recollected how she, a UCLA college graduate in sociology, worked under civil service at City Hall in the Bureau of Identification. "As soon as the war started," she explained, "they didn't want any more Japanese Americans in City Hall. They transferred us for a six-week temporary position, and I was sent to the Citizens Branch Library as a librarian. They said it would be for six weeks and then we were terminated." Again, discrimination took over.

Mitamura Kodama recalled her first college semester. "I didn't even finish. I felt like people were turning their heads and looking at me with different looks; I just didn't feel comfortable. So I quit." Racism eroded the academic environment for her.

Facing the difficulties at the time, Mitamura Kodama concluded that "there was no way I could change anything except within myself." In this inner search she sees herself blessed. In addition, we can sense an inward strength, a quiet commitment that "camp" will never happen again. The Japanese American Citizens League of Imperial Valley in which she is an active member strives to insure that "camp" will not reoccur. "If there were any signs of it, they'd immediately address it. We benefit from their actions." Mitamura Kodama's support for the Imperial Valley Japanese American Gallery also shows her dedication to tradition. "Basically, it's to honor our parents and their work and values that they instilled in all of us," she concluded.

In camp, Ruri Tsuchiya Ishimaru pointed out that "at the beginning, all camp instructors, they thought Japanese are uneducated... but they found out that most were college graduates or college students. Japanese standards very high." These illustrations reflect the racism which Ruri Tsuchiya Ishimaru observed. Tasting the bitterness of camp, Kawashima Ota, Tsuchiya Ishimaru, and Shigematsu Hoshizaki, all three, experienced discrimination and commented on it.

Gender inequity existed in camp, too. Women in camp were paid $16.00 a month. The chef, newspaper editor, and a few other select positions received $19.00 a month. However, only men held these positions, Ruri Tsuchiya Ishimaru noted. In contrast, European American staff earned $167.00 a month.

Mitamura Sanbonmatsu had conflicted feelings about camp, the lack of amenities, having to walk everywhere, and not having books in school. Still she remembered the dances. Before camp, she, at age fifteen, still lived in a sheltered environment, interacting with friends and an extended Japanese family. Thus, Mitamura Sanbonmatsu can recall some of the good times in camp.

Interestingly, Mitamura Sanbonmatsu did not focus on discrimination. Was anything left unsaid or perhaps her life spanned only fifteen years before camp in contrast with the older women interviewed?

For some, camp may be a reference point. Certainly this was true for Mabel Kawashima Ota. She had transcended camp and moved on when she made a decision to go back to school and get her teaching credentials. The unfolding of knowledge about her baby that something was wrong, that her daughter had brain damage, spurred her on to return to college. Later she read in a newspaper that the first Japanese American teacher had been hired in Los Angeles. She applied and got the job. In 1962 she became the first Asian American woman principal in California.

Resettlement, Discrimination and Redress

Moving on beyond camp—resettlement was really very difficult. To deny Japanese Americans, a collective group, rather than an individualistic group, the possibility of returning to the West Coast where they had put down roots before the war; to ban Japanese Americans from walking in groups down the street; and to deny them from moving into a community together with other Japanese American families, was to deny a dominant feature of their culture: *groupness.* It was utilized to separate and make invisible Japanese Americans. Recovery and healing often happen in community. In this situation, community was denied. Only eight families returned to Imperial Valley, whereas before the war, over 2000 Japanese and Japanese Americans lived there.[4]

Shigematsu Hoshizaki before camp had graduated from Woodbury College in Los Angeles, majoring in clothing design and millinery. She had also learned Japanese cultural traditions. She married, and she and her spouse, George, had a popular pool hall with a soda fountain. Upon their return to El Centro after camp, they could not successfully resume their business. There was a great deal of discrimination. No doubt, this was due to the government's admonition to *not* return to Imperial County upon leaving camp. "One never forgets camp," she commented. Consequently, the pool hall and soda fountain under the ownership of Shigematsu Hoshizaki never again flourished. Each woman reflected on the turning points in her life and shared stories that were passed down to them.

In 1981, public hearings were held by the Commission of Wartime Relocation and Internment of Civilians across the United States. Kawashima Ota testified and commented it was one of the most difficult things she had ever had to do. In 1988, the government issued a formal apology to each Japanese American interned. The Redress Movement led by the Japanese American Citizens League (JACL), successfully challenged the government to pay each survivor of the camps $20,000 and the 1988 Civil Liberties Law was signed into law. All of the other interviewees in some way supported the redress movement and continued working to keep the memory of internment alive through participation in the Japanese American Citizens League, "Poston Reunions," Japanese American Gallery in the Imperial Valley Pioneers' Museum and through many other "Remembrance" activities.

Transcendence

Indeed, these five young women confronted camp and moved through it and beyond. Early life before camp contrasts with rampant racism and hysteria, and fear surrounding the transport and arrival, along with the frustration, depression, lack of privacy, and amenities in camp. Barbed wire, watch towers, miserable food, and lack of the familiar increased the alienation and discomfort. Add to this the constant discrimination upon leaving camp reflected in their stories. Moreover, the dust storms became forever stamped in the memories of these five women. They overcame the psychological, social, and economic wounds of evacuation, incarceration and hostile homecoming with the spirit of *gambaru:* withstanding adversity, gaining respect and acceptance.

Metaphors of these five women emerged. Mabel Kawashima Ota, in her interview, talked about the seeds of morning glories she planted in camp outside her barrack door; when those purple morning glories bloomed, her heart stirred and memories of home hovered about her.

Tsuchiya Ishimaru remembered that when the trees were planted and grew, the meadowlarks would come, their songs like flutes playing—musical, and sweet. She saw hope, strength and courage of the Japanese American people—the resilience of the human spirit.

The stories of triumph of these five Imperial Valley women give us lessons of inspiration: to live through camp and survive, to start over, to develop new lives, successful and rewarding. These five Nisei women have, indeed, the resiliency of the transcendent spirit.

NOTES

Works frequently cited have been identified by the following abbreviations:

Abbreviations for Repositories

Cornell Poston Collection, #3830	Cornell University, Ithaca, NY. Japanese American Relocation Centers Record Collection 1935-1953, #3830 is housed in the Department of Manuscripts and University Archives. It contains 39 boxes of materials on Poston I, including papers, journal entries, photos, watercolor paintings and drawings, reports, newspaper clippings, and interviews in the Rare Manuscript Collections at the Carl A. Krock Library at Cornell University. Some of the classified materials have been declassified as of August 26, 2003.
Fullerton Japanese American Project	California State University Oral History Program. Fullerton, California. Japanese American Project.
National Archives	National Archives, Washington, DC.

Introduction

1. Lucie Hirata, "Testimony to the National Commission on Wartime Relocation and Internment of Civilians." These hearings were held in Los Angeles. Statement on Behalf of UCLA Asian American Studies Centre (Washington, DC: National Archives, August 6, 1981), 3.
2. Lane Ryo Hirabayashi and James A. Hirabayashi, "Behind Barbed Wire," in *The View From Within,* ed. Karin M. Higa (Los Angeles: The Japanese American National Museum, the UCLA Wight Art Gallery, and the UCLA Asian American Studies Center, 1992), 52.

3. Vincent Tajiri, ed., *Through Innocent Eyes* (Los Angeles, California: Keiro Services Press, 1990), 40.
4. Agnes Savilla, Oral History Interview, Interviewer: David Hacker (Fullerton, California: California State University Oral History Program. Japanese American Project, April 8, 1978), 2.
5. Savilla, Oral History Interview, 3.
6. Savilla, Oral History Interview, 3.
7. Savilla, Oral History Interview, 2.
8. Savilla, Oral History Interview, 5.
9. Savilla, Oral History Interview, 4.
10. Savilla, Oral History Interview, 6.
11. Akira Loveridge-Sanbonmatsu, "Poston: Bitter and Sweet Memories." Speech Presented at the Japanese American Poston Reunion, Los Angeles, October 25, 1997 in *Poston I—1942-1997—55 Year Camp Reunion* (Costa Mesa, California: Worthington Reunions, Fall 1997), 1-5.
12. Savilla, Oral History Interview, 9.
13. Sue Kunitomi Embrey, Arthur A. Hansen, and Betty Kulberg Mitson, *Manzanar Martyr: An Interview with Harry Y. Ueno* (Fullerton, California: Oral History Program, Japanese American Project, 1986), 5.
14. Valeri Matsumoto, "Windows on a World," *The Women's Review of Books* VI, no. 10-11 (July 1989): 5.

Chapter 1: Mabel Kawashima Ota's Story

1. Mabel Kawashima Ota, "Testimony to the National Commission on Wartime Relocation and Internment of Civilians." These hearings were held in Los Angeles. (Washington, DC: National Archives, July 7, 1981), 2-3.
2. Kawashima Ota, "Testimony…," 2-4.
3. By the end of 1943, camps "were producing 85 percent of the vegetables they consumed." See Mei Nakano, *Japanese American Women* (Berkeley, California: Mina Press Publishing, 1990), 145.

Chapter 2: In Mary Shigematsu Hoshizaki's Own Words

1. Minutes, Women's Club Meeting, July 16, 1942, Cornell Poston Collection #3830, Box 8, File 19, 1-2.
2. Minutes, Joint Meeting of Ha Ha No Kai (Mother's Club) and Fujin Kai (Women's Club), July 18, 1942, Cornell Poston Collection #3830, Box 8, File 19, 1-3.

3. "Poston I Fujin Kai," Summary Report, May 1943, Cornell Poston Collection #3830, Box 8, File 21, 7.
4. Summary Report, May 1943, Cornell Poston Collection #3830, Box 8, File 21, 9-10.
5. Minutes, Women's Clubs Quad Chair, September 29, 1942, Cornell Poston Collection #3830, Box 8, File 19, 1-2.
6. Poston Fujin Kai Women's Club Notes, July 16, 1943, Cornell Poston Collection #3830, Box 8, File 20.
7. Journal Excerpt of Henry Sigura, July 23, 1942, Cornell Poston Collection #3830, Box 8, File 11.
8. Journal Entry of Elmer Tanigoshi, July 29, 1942, Cornell Poston Collection #3830, Box 8, File 36.
9. Journal Excerpt of Yoshiko Kubo, July 23, 1942, Cornell Poston Collection #3830, Box 8, File 11.
10. Journal Entry of Yoshiko Kubo, July 24, 1942, Cornell Poston Collection #3830, Box 8, File 11.
11. Journal Excerpt of F.M., July 24, 1942, Cornell Poston Collection #3830, Box 8, File 11.
12. Journal Entry of F.M., July 24, 1942, Cornell Poston Collection, #3830, Box 8, File 11.
13. Journal Excerpt of Seizo Sakamoto, July 23, 1942, Cornell Poston Collection, #3830, Box 8, File 11.
14. Journal Entry. (No name), July 22 (n.d., probably 1942), Cornell Poston Collection #3830, Box 8, File 11.
15. Brian Niiya, "Internment Chronology," in *The View From Within,* ed. Karin M. Higa, rev. ed. (Los Angeles: Japanese American National Museum, UCLA Wight Art Gallery and the UCLA Asian American Studies Center, 1994), 62.
16. Shelia Hamanaka, *The Journey* (New York: Orchard Books, 1990), 27.
17. Jason Jackson, Conversations about Mary Shigematsu Hoshizaki, his grandmother, by phone, April, 2000 and at the Imperial Valley Japanese American Reunion Dinner in Holtville, California, March 2, 2002 and Imperial Valley Japanese American Citizen League Recognition Dinner and Weekend in El Centro, California, April 29-May 1, 2005.

Chapter 3: Mary Mitamura Sanbonmatsu's Narrative

1. Fifty-four buildings including six auditoriums were built for and by the residents of the three Poston camps, the only internment center residents permitted to construct school buildings. " 'Women worked continuously, intelligently, and worked well,' " according to the construction engineer, Charles A. Popkin. See Ruth Okimoto, *Sharing a Desert Home* (Berkeley, California: Heyday Books, 2001), 11-12.
2. *Papers*, October 12, 1942, Cornell Poston Collection #3830, Box 8, File 3.
3. Cary Report, May 12, 1943, Cornell Poston Collection #3830, Box 8, File 39, 6.
4. Cary Report, May 12, 1943, Cornell Poston Collection #3830, Box 8, File 39, 5-6.

5. Cary Report, May 12, 1943, Cornell Poston collection #3830, Box 8, File 39, 4.
6. "The Educational Program at Poston, Arizona," January, 1943, Cornell Poston Collection #3830, Box 8, File 39, 2, 5.
7. Cary Report, January, 1943, Cornell Poston Collection #3830, Box 8, File 39, 2.
8. Educational Council, Poston I, II, III [Camps] Minutes, February 26, 1943, Cornell Poston Collection #3830, Box 8, File 39, 2.
9. Poston Senior High School Curriculum Bulletin, 1943-1944, Cornell Poston Collection #3830, Box 9, File 6, 3.
10. "Guidance and Evaluation in the Poston Schools, 1942-1943 Report," August 1943, Cornell Poston Collection #3830, Box 9, File 6, n.p.n. (possibly page 4).
11. Personal and Family Information Form, 1942-1943, Cornell Poston Collection #3830, Box 9, File 6, 1-4.
12. *Post-Año 1944*, Poston I High School Yearbook of Mary Mitamura, n.p.n.
13. *Post-Año 1944*, Poston I High School Yearbook of Mary Mitamura, n.p.n.
14. Journal Excerpt of Henry Sigura, July 23, 1942, Cornell Poston Collection #3830, Box 8, File 11.
15. William C. Rhoden, "When Baseball Could Provide a Way Out," *New York Times*, February 27, 1995, sec. c, 3.

Chapter 4: Yoshiko Mitamura Kodama's Oral History

1. "Mitamura Kodama Nuptial," *Poston City Page*, July 21, 1943. Cited by George Kodama, "Executive Order 9066, Evacuation of All People of Japanese American Descent from West Coast" (Research Paper, June 5, 1992), 13.
2. A.H. Leighton Report, July 10, 1943, Cornell Poston Collection #3830, Box 1, file 33, 1, 9. Dr. Leighton is a sociologist, psychiatrist, anthropologist and educator. His book, *The Governing of Men*, a definitive book is based on Poston I Camp.
3. The four cases of Mitsuye Endo, Gordon Hirabayashi, Fred Korematsu and Minoru Yasui are discussed in detail. These four court cases challenged the government's actions of mass removal of 120,000 Japanese and Japanese Americans and placing them in "concentration camps" in the United States. See Brian Niiya, ed., *Japanese American History* (Los Angeles, California: The Japanese American National Museum, 1993), 17-19, 175-176.
4. In 1988, Congress enacted The Civil Liberties Act granting redress to the victims of internment. The commission's findings declared that the causes were "race prejudice, war hysteria and a failure of political leadership." See *Personal Justice Denied*, Report of the Commission on Wartime Relocation and Internment of Civilians, Second Edition (Seattle, Washington: University of Seattle Press, 1992), 459.

Chapter 5: Ruri Tsuchiya Ishimaru's Life Story

1. D.L. Myer, "Japanese Americans Educated in Japan," "The Kibei," January 28, 1944, Cornell Poston Collection #3830, Box 1, File 28, 5.
2. Ruri Tsuchiya's primary language was Japanese. In Japan, she studied French and German. English was her second language in the United States.
3. D.L. Myer, "Kibei," Report, Community Analysis Section, January 28, 1944, Cornell Poston Collection #3830, Box 1, File 28, 7.
4. A.H. Leighton, "Monthly Report on the Colorado River War Relocation Center for Evacuated Japanese," July 10, 1943, Cornell Poston Collection #3830, Box 1, File 33, 3.
5. Toshio Yatsushiro and Iwao Ishino, "Resettling the West Coast Evacuees," Part II, February 21, 1944, Cornell Poston Collection #3830, Box 11, File 10, 5.
6. Yatsushiro and Ishino, Part III, 6.
7. Yatsushiro and Ishino, Part III, 7.
8. Yatsushiro and Ishino, Part III, 9.
9. Yatsushiro and Ishino, Part III, 3-3a.
10. Mikio understood and spoke only Japanese until he entered preschool where he stopped speaking Japanese. His parents spoke to him in Japanese so he understands it, according to Mikio and Vickie Ishimaru.
11. Mikio now has his own law firm with Vickie assisting.
12. *Personal Justice Denied*, Report of the Commission on Wartime Relocation and Internment of Civilians, Second Edition (Seattle, Washington: University of Seattle Press, 1992), 167.
13. "Organization charts hanging on office walls conspicuously reserved all top positions for 'white men'." See Alexander Leighton, *The Governing of Men* (Princeton, New Jersey: Princeton University Press, 1945), 107.

Chapter 6: The Transcendent Spirit

1. Toshio Yatsushiro and Iwao Ishino, "Resettling the West Coast Evacuees," Part I, February 28, 1944, Cornell Poston Collection #3830, Box 11, File 10, 5.
2. Kiku Hori Funabi, *"Gambaru," Bridge* 7, no. 4 (Winter 1981-1982): 18.
3. Brian Niiya, "Internment Chronology," in *The View From Within*, ed. Karin M. Higa, ed., rev. ed. (LosAngeles: Japanese American National Museum, 1994), 62.
4. Mikio Ishimaru, "Ruri Ishimaru, A Personal History," 1998, 6.

Works Cited

Embrey, Sue Kunitomi, Arthur A. Hansen, and Betty Kulberg Mitson. *Manzanar Martyr: An Interview with Harry Y. Ueno*. Fullerton, California: Oral History Program, Japanese American Project, 1986.

Funabi, Kiku Hori. "Gambaru." *Bridge* 7, no. 4. (Winter 1981-1982): 18.

Hamanaka, Sheila. *The Journey*. New York: Orchard Books, 1990.

Hirabayashi, Lane Ryo and James A. Hirabayashi. "Behind Barbed Wire" in *The View From Within*. Edited by Karin M. Higa. Los Angeles: The Japanese American National Museum, the UCLA Wight Art Gallery, and the UCLA Asian American Studies Center, 1992.

Hirata, Lucie. "Testimony to the National Commission on Wartime Relocation and Internment of Civilians." Held in Los Angeles. Statement on Behalf of UCLA Asian American Studies Centre. Washington, DC: National Archives, August 6, 1981: 3.

Ishimaru, Mikio. "Ruri Ishimaru, A Personal History." 1998.

Ishimaru, Stone. *Colorado River Relocation Center*. Los Angeles, CA: Tec Com Productions, 1987.

Jackson, Jason. Conversations about Mary Shigematsu Hoshizaki, his grandmother by phone, April, 2000 and at the Imperial Valley Japanese American Reunion Dinner in Holtville, California, March 2, 2002 and at the Imperial Valley Japanese American Citizens League Recognition Dinner and Weekend April 29-May 1, 2005 in El Centro.

Japanese American Relocation Centers Records Collection, 1935-1953, #3830. Collection is housed in the Department of Manuscripts and University Archives, Cornell University Libraries. It contains 39 boxes of materials on Poston, including papers, journal entries, photos, watercolor paintings and drawings, reports, newspaper clippings, and interviews in the Rare Manuscript Collections at the Carl A. Krock Library at Cornell University. Some of the classified materials have been declassified as of August 26, 2003.

Kawashima Ota, Mabel. Audio Recorded Oral History Interview, April 6, 1994. Follow-up interviews and conversations, Los Angeles, October 24, 1997, August 29, 2000 and February 2002.

Kawashima Ota, Mabel. "Testimony to the National Commission on Wartime Relocation and Internment of Civilians." Held in Los Angeles. Washington, DC: National Archives, July 7, 1981.

Kodama, George. "Executive Order 9066, Evacuation of All People of Japanese American Descent from West Coast." A Research Paper, June 5, 1992.

Leighton, Alexander. *The Governing of Men*. Princeton, New Jersey: Princeton University Press, 1945.

Loveridge-Sanbonmatsu, Akira. Participant in a Poston strike, November, 1942.

---. "Poston: Bitter and Sweet Memories." Speech Presented at the Japanese American Poston Reunion held in Los Angeles, October 25, 1997 in *Poston I—1942-1997—55 Year Camp Reunion*. Costa Mesa, California: Worthington Reunions, 1997.

Matsumoto, Valeri. "Windows on a World." *The Women's Review of Books* 6, no. 10-11 (July 1989): 5.

Mitamura Sanbonmatsu, Mary. Audio Recorded Oral History Interview, April 10, 1994. Follow-up interviews and conversations in El Centro and Holtville, California, October 27-28, 1997, February 2002, April 28—May 1, 2005, Fall 2005-Winter 2006.

---. Personal Interview. Encinitas, California, July 23-24, 1989.

Mitamura Kodama, Yoshiko. Audio Recorded Oral History Interview, April 10, 1994. Follow-up Interview and conversations in El Centro, California, October 28, 1997 and April 29—30, 2005.

"Mitamura Kodama Nuptial." *Poston City Page*, July 21, 1943.

"A More Perfect Union," National Exhibition of the Japanese American Internment. Smithsonian Museum. Washington, DC, April 1994.

Nakano, Mei. *Japanese American Women*. Berkeley, California: Mina Press, 1990.

Niiya, Brian. "Internment Chronology." *The View From Within*. ed. Karin M. Higa. First Edition Revised. Los Angeles: Japanese American National Museum, 1994.

Niiya, Brian, ed. *Japanese American History*. Los Angeles: The Japanese American National Museum, 1993.

Okimoto, Ruth. *Sharing a Desert Home.* Berkeley, CA: Heyday Books, 2001.

Personal Justice Denied. Report of the Commission on Wartime Relocation and Internment of Civilians. Second Edition. Seattle, Washington: University of Seattle Press, 1992.

Post-Año, 1944. Poston I High School Yearbook of Mary Mitamura.

Rhoden, William C. "When Baseball Could Provide a Way Out." *New York Times*, 27 February 1995: section c.

Savilla, Agnes. Oral History Interview. Interviewer: David A. Hacker. Fullerton, California: California State University Oral History Program. Japanese American Project. April 8, 1978: 2.

Shigematsu Hoshizaki, Mary. Oral History Interview, April 18, 1994. Follow-up Interviews, April 13, 1997, April 17, 1997, and October 27, 1997, in El Centro, California. Conversations by phone and correspondence. March 25, 27, 29 and April 2, 27 and May 2, 2000.

Tajiri, Vincent, ed. *Through Innocent Eyes*. Los Angeles, California: Keiro Services Press, 1990.

Tateishi, John. "Mabel Ota." *And Justice for All*. New York: Random House, 1999.

Tsuychia Ishimaru, Ruri. Audio Recorded Oral History Interview I, Heiwa Terrace, Chicago, July 24, 1983.

---. Oral History Interview II, Chicago, Spring, 1992.

---. Audio Recorded Oral History Interview III, Chicago, March 19, 1994.

---. Follow-up conversations over the years until her death in 1997.

Yatsushiro, Toshio and Iwao Ishino. "Resettling the West Coast Evacuees." A report in Four Parts. Part I: February 28, 1944; Part II: February 21, 1994; Part III: February 16, 1944; Part IV: March 13, 1944. Third Draft. Cornell Poston Collection #3830, Box 11, File 10. (These writers were members of the Sociological Research Project of the Colorado River War Relocation Center, Poston, Arizona. They received additional training in public opinion measurement at the National Opinion Research Center.)

Selected Works and Resources Consulted

Asamen, Tim. Chair and Coordinator of the Japanese American Gallery in the Imperial Valley Pioneers' Museum from 1991 to the present. He served on the Imperial County Historical Society (ICHS) Board of Directors 1997-2004. In addition, Asamen served as President of the ICHS in 2001 as well as on the Executive Board (1999-2004).

Atkinson, Paul, Amanda Coffey, Sara Delamont, John Lofland and Lyn Lofland, eds. *Handbook of Ethnography*. Thousand Oaks, California: Sage Publications, Inc., 2002.

Estes, Donald H. and Matthew T. Estes. "Further and Further Away…" *The Journal of San Diego History*, 39, 1-2 (Winter-Spring 1993).

Funakoshi, Candice. Follow up conversations about her mother, Mabel Kawashima Ota, Fall 2005-Spring, 2006.

Gesensway, Deborah and Mindy Roseman. *Beyond Words: Images from America's Concentration Camps.* Ithaca, New York: Cornell University Press, 1987.

Gluck, Sherna Berger and Daphne Patai. *Women's Words: The Feminist Practice of Oral History*. New York: Routledge, Chapman and Hall, Inc., 1991.

Heidlebaugh, Nola J. *Judgement, Rhetoric and the Problem of Incommensurability.* Columbia, South Carolina: University of South Carolina Press, 2001.

Ichioka, Yuji, ed. *Views from Within*. Los Angeles, California: Asian American Studies Center, University of California at Los Angeles, 1989.

Iki, Darcie. "Asking Questions, Changing Lives: The Value of Oral History." *Japanese American National Museum Quarterly* 11, 2 (Summer 1996): 3-7. The entire issue is devoted to oral history.

Imahori, T. Todd. "Revisiting the Responses 50 Years Later: Identity Management of 'Yes-Yes' and 'No-No' Boys." A Paper presented at Speech Communication Association Conference. San Diego, November 1996.

Kimura, Lillian. (President of the Japanese American Citizens League in 1994). Response letter to my query to locate Mabel Kawashima Ota. February 25, 1994.

Loveridge-Sanbonmatsu, Akira. "A Desert Harvested." Syracuse, New York: May Memorial Unitarian Universalist Society, 1983.

---. "Desert Poppies After the Storm: Internment Camp from 1942-45," Syracuse, New York: May Memorial Unitarian Universalist Society, March 2004.

Loveridge-Sanbonmatsu, Joan. "Behind Barbed Wire: Ruri Ishimaru." A Paper Presented at Quest, A Research Conference at Oswego State University, Oswego, NY, April 8, 1992.

---. "Nationalism, Racism, and Japanese American Women in World War II: The Transcendent Spirit." An Invited International Public Lecture. Tokyo University, Japan, May 1997.

---. "Oral History and Poetry: Two Forms of Women's Discourse for Inspired Teaching and Writing." A Paper Presented at New York Women's Studies Association Annual Conference. Russell Sage College, Troy, NY, March 15-17, 1991.

---. "Women's Voices from the Japanese American Camps." A Paper Presented at a Women's Studies Symposium, Oswego State University, Oswego, NY, February 1991.

---. "World War II Internment Camps through the Lens of Japanese American Women: Oral Histories and Interviews." A Paper Presented at the American Historical Association 105 Annual Meeting. New York City, December 27-30, 1990.

Madison, D. Soyini. *Critical Ethnography.* Thousand Oaks, California. Sage Publications, Inc. 2005.

"Make I.V. [Imperial Valley] Japanese History Alive." *Tekoku Helgen News Issue* 5 (January 1993).

Matsuoka, Jack. *Camp II, Block 211.* Japan: Japan Publications, Inc., 1974.

Spradley, J.P. *The Ethnographic Interview.* New York: Holt, Rinehart & Winston, 1979.

Takaki, Ronald. *Strangers from a Different Shore.* NY: Back Bay Books, 1998.

Tamura, Linda. *The Hood River Issei.* Illinois: University of Illinois, 1993.

Tonai, Rosalyn and Chizu Iiyama, eds. *Oral History Guide.* San Francisco: National Japanese American Historical Society, 1993.

Tsuruda, Gerald K., Terry Ishimaru Itano, Fran F. Nakumura, and Fred S. Okimoto. *The Road Not Forgotten: The Journey of Japanese Descendents in Butte, Colusa, Sutter, and Yuba Counties (1889-1995)*. Sacramento: Tom's Printing, Inc., and Marysville Chapter Japanese American Citizens League, 1995.

Wieder, Alan. "Oral History and Questions of Interaction for Educational Historians." *International Journal of Oral History* 10, no. 3 (November 1989): 131-38.

Yamada, Jeni. "Legacy of Silence (II)." In *Last Witnesses Reflections on the Wartime Internment of Japanese Americans,* edited by Erica Harth. NY: Palgrave Publisher Ltd., 2001.

Yamada, Mitsuye. *Camp Notes*. California: Shameless Hussy Press, 1976.

---. "The Cult of the 'Perfect' Language; Censorship by Class, Gender and Race." *Sowing Ti Leaves*, edited by Mitsuye Yamada and Sarie Sachie Hylkema. California: Multi-Cultural Women Writers, 1990.

---. *Desert Run*. Latham, New York: Kitchen Table: Women of Color Press, 1988.

---. "Legacy of Silence (I)." In *Last Witnesses Reflections on the Wartime Internment of Japanese Americans*, edited by Erica Harth. NY: Palgrave Publishers Ltd., 2001.

Wellman, Judith. *The Road to Seneca Falls*. Urbana and Chicago: University of Illinois Press, 2004.

About the Author

JOAN LOVERIDGE-SANBONMATSU, Ph.D., is Professor Emerita of Communication Studies and Women's Studies, and Summer Sessions Faculty for the Intensive English Program at Oswego State University in Oswego, New York. She has been doing research on the Japanese American Internment at Poston since 1983 and incorporated this research in her courses, Intercultural Communication and the Political Discourse of Contemporary Movements, Female-Male Communication, Women's Studies, and Intensive English.

The research for this book centers on oral histories of Japanese American women interned at Poston, Arizona, the Cornell University Archives which houses thirty-nine boxes of materials on Poston, California University at Fullerton Oral History Program and the National Archives. She was involved in working toward a multicultural curriculum for many years and initiated the first course in Intercultural Communication in the SUNY system. She has given many presentations on integrating multicultural issues into the curriculum, as well as on Japanese American women at Poston, locally, nationally, and internationally. Married to Akira Loveridge-Sanbonmatsu, interned in Poston I for over three years, they with their two sons have visited Poston and attended various Poston Reunions. Her Ph.D. from The Pennsylvania State University focused on the study of political discourse and social change and history.

Mark Knopp

Her publications include: *Feminism and Woman's Life* (co-author); *Women Public Speakers in the U.S., 1925-1993*, Vol. 2, (contributing author); *Why Don't You Talk Right? Multicultural Communication Perspectives* (contributing author); *Life in a Fishbowl: A Call to Serve* (contributing author); *Winged Odyssey: Poems and Stories*, author; contributing poet to publications; contributing author to professional journals including *Howard Journal of Communications*, *Communication Education* and *Phoebe*; poetry editor/editorial board: *Lake Effect*, 1985-1992.

Joan Loveridge-Sanbonmatsu is a member of the Japanese American Citizens League, New York Chapter, the Imperial County Historical Society, Poets and Writers, Inc., National Communication Association, and National Women's Studies Association, among others.

Editors

Akira Loveridge-Sanbonmatsu, Associate Professor Emerita, State University of New York at Brockport. Interned at Poston I for more than three years, he has spoken throughout the United States, and Puerto Rico on the *camps.*

Nancy Seale Osborne, writer, editor, poet, author of *Crazy Quilt: Funky Smalltown Texas and Pieces of Life* (Hale Mary Press) and *In the Shadow of a Miracle* (Hale Mary Press). She is a professor emerita as librarian and archivist at the State University of New York at Oswego. As a grandmother, she continues to canoe and paint watercolors.

Rosabel A. Wang, Director and Systems Analyst for the International Bibliography of Theatre and Dance project. This project is now under the auspices of EBSCO Publishing which offers the database within its Academic Search Premier.

Design and Illustrations

Elizabeth Percival is a senior designer in the publications office at Syracuse University. She has designed several books for local authors and in her free time enjoys traveling, gardening and cooking.